BATTLE TALES
FROM
BURMA

BATTLE TALES

FROM

BURMA

by

John Randle

Pen & Sword

MILITARY

First published in Great Britain in 2004 by
Pen & Sword Military
an imprint of
Pen & Sword Books Ltd
47 Church Street
Barnsley
South Yorkshire
S70 2AS

ISBN 1 84415 112 3

A CIP catalogue record for this book is
available from the British Library

Typeset in Sabon by
Phoenix Typesetting, Auldgirth, Dumfriesshire

Printed and bound in England by
CPI UK

Pen & Sword Books Ltd incorporates the imprints of Pen & Sword
Aviation, Pen & Sword Maritime, Pen & Sword Military, Wharncliffe
Local History, Pen & Sword Select, Pen & Sword Military Classics and
Leo Cooper.

For a complete list of Pen & Sword titles please contact
PEN & SWORD BOOKS LIMITED
47 Church Street, Barnsley, South Yorkshire, S70 2AS, England
E-mail: enquiries@pen-and-sword.co.uk
Website: www.pen-and-sword.co.uk

To all those soldiers of the Seventh Battalion
The (10th) Baluch Regiment
who served in the Burma Campaign
(1942–1945).

Contents

FOREWORD

By

The Rt. Hon. The Viscount Slim

World War Two produced the largest volunteer Army of nearly three million soldiers from the then Indian Empire. Without it Great Britain and her Allies would have had difficulty in mustering sufficient forces to defeat the Germans, their Italian allies, and the Japanese Empire.

By 1945 this great Old Indian Army recruited across its Subcontinent from the numerous martial tribes, of all religions and cultures, had proved itself in battle and greatly enhanced its fighting reputation in the major Theatres of the War.

Success came from the courage, loyalty, discipline and the resolute fighting qualities of the Indian Soldier. Above all by the inspired leadership of his British and Indian Officers together with their Viceroy Commissioned Officers. A unique combination of successful leadership.

John Randle writes with gentle affectionate pride of his Indian Soldiers in the famous Baluch Regiment. He is perhaps overly modest in describing the many ferocious close-quarter encounters and battles in which he lead his men. To survive some four years of almost constant action may be lucky, but it takes and becomes a true warrior leader to turn and turn again towards an enemy as brave, stubborn and vicious as the Jap.

This personal and special book gives the reader pause to ponder and learn, particularly how very fortunate The Old Indian Army was to have so many outstanding Officers like the Author.

SLIM
House of Lords
2004

Acknowledgements

As in any literary venture, even of this modest nature, the author has to be warmly grateful for the help, advice and encouragement of a number of people.

Principal among these is Charles Coubrough, comrade-in-arms, old friend and author of a fine wartime book himself. His encouragement to publish what was originally intended as a private piece of writing, and his practical help and advice have been invaluable; without it, this book would never have been published.

Similar warm thanks must go to Major General Colin Shortis, regimental friend from the Devonshire and Dorset Regiment, whose encouragement, wisdom and practical help with the manuscript have been invaluable, and to John Nunneley, friend and "old Burma Hand" who took so much trouble to help me polish up the manuscript and whose literary and publishing experience have been so supportive. I am grateful too to General John Wilsey, another Devon and Dorset regimental friend, for his introduction to Brigadier Henry Wilson of Pen and Sword Publications, who has skilfully combined the role of business-like publisher and helpful counsellor.

My gratitude also goes to Lord Slim, President of the Burma Star Association and of course the soldier son of our inspiring leader in Burma, General, later Field Marshal, "Bill" Slim, for so kindly writing an undeservedly generous Foreword.

I am most grateful to Clifford Martin, Tommy Bruin and Roderick MacLean, friends and fellow 7th Baluchis, with help on facts and dates and general advice.

Profound thanks are due to Mrs Chris Dare, who, after years deciphering my appalling handwriting at Regimental Headquarters of the Devonshire and Dorset Regiment, has, in her retirement, been a tower of strength with her immaculate typing.

Finally, but of the greatest significance, I acknowledge with deep gratitude all the encouragement that my wife Peggy gave me to write the original manuscript in the early 90s and before the sad onset of Alzheimer's Disease.

July 2003

Preface

I originally wrote these stories some years ago for a very limited private circulation to family and close friends, who have now encouraged me to publish them. I naturally gave much thought – and took advice – as to how I should present them. In the first place there is a very full account of my battalion's fighting in the History of the Baluch Regiment in WW2, and I certainly did not wish to appear to be writing another. Secondly, there have been plenty of books about the Burma fighting – Japanese Banzai bayonet attacks, close-quarter fighting, bloodshed and the horrors of war – and though I did have my fair share of these, I wanted to avoid taking that well-trodden path. So, rather than write a conventional and continuous memoir, I decided to recount a collection of separate stories, some serious and some lighthearted, some quite long and some mere vignettes. I then ran into a snag. When I first wrote them, thirteen years ago, it was essential to make each story complete within itself, and this became even more important when a number of them were published separately in service journals. This obviously involved setting out a short introductory paragraph of the general background to each story. It was also important to keep the story concise and to the point, and avoid digression into extraneous background, particularly of personalities, and I have decided to maintain that literary discipline rather than completely rehash them to the detriment of the balance of the story. It does mean, however, that there is occasionally some minor repetition, for which I ask the reader's forbearance.

However, an infantryman's war is, above all, about men. I then realized that, in striving for succinctness, it might seem that I was not interested in the men of all ranks who were my comrades-in-arms and friends, even though they were a fundamental part of my life in those far-off days, and, despite the years, in many cases, remain so still. I have therefore given at Appendix A a profile of everyone mentioned in the stories, so that the reader who may be interested can see how fortunate I was. I have also interspersed the stories with an occasional brief "Background Events", so that they can be viewed chronologically against the wider and relevant part of the long-drawn-out Burma Campaign.

Whilst I have always retained the copyright of my stories, courtesy requires me to acknowledge, with my thanks, the editors of *Dekho*, the journal of the Burma Star Association, of the Newsletter of the Indian Army Association (IAA), of *Durbar*, the journal of the Indian Military Historical Society, and of the Journal of the Devonshire & Dorset Regiment for the compliment that they paid me in publishing my stories. The same goes to the Editor of *Tales from the Burma Campaign*, published by the Burma Campaign Fellowship Group.

The basic facts of every story are, as far as I can honestly recall, true. Obviously when writing from memory about events which took place well over half a century ago I may have got some of the dates, places and matters of detail wrong, and the same goes for any conversation recorded verbatim.

The obvious dangers of any autobiographical writing, especially about war, are the opportunities it gives to be critical of those with whose opinions and actions one disagreed. There is an equal danger of depicting one's own motives and actions, even unintentionally, on a rather higher level than they actually were. I have always deplored those, other than genuine biographers, who, years after events, write disparagingly and unkindly about people for no other apparent reason than spite or attempting to pay off old scores. I have no old scores to settle and I have tried to refrain from criticism of others. Where the whole point of the story depends on the character of an individual, I have obviously brought out weaknesses or idiosyncrasies, but I have also endeavoured to highlight that person's good qualities. I have equally tried to be honest about my own shortcomings, on many occasions.

There is one central thread to this rag-bag of reminiscences, one which every British officer who ever had the privilege of commanding men of the old Indian Army in battle would assuredly confirm, and that is the always sustaining, and often uplifting, strength we derived from the unfailing loyalty, courage, uncomplaining and cheerful endurance in hardship and comradeship of the men we led. It is something that I look back on down the years with unforgettable gratitude and humility.

INTRODUCTION

My original aim in life, in those long-ago imperial days before WWII, was to get into the Indian Political Service, the junior partner of the Indian Civil Service, which dealt with the North-West Frontier and the princely states. Entry was via the Indian Police or the Indian Army, and Colonel "Boomer" Barrett, a legendary Baluch officer and friend of my father, had undertaken to help me to get a nomination for this much sought-after regiment. I had passed the entry exam for Sandhurst in the summer of 1939 with the aim of entering in January 1940. However, in the autumn of 1939 Sandhurst was closed for the training of officers for regular commissions, and so when, in 1940, the India Office/War Office started looking for wartime officers for a planned expansion of the Indian Army I was written to. This was before the days of War Office Selection Boards (WOSBs) and the selection of potential officers was made on the rough and ready basis principally of a public school education, Certificate A in the school Officers' Training Corps (OTC) and a short interview with an Indian Army Colonel in the India Office. I duly cleared this hurdle and at the end of 1940 joined a party of several hundred other public school boys at Aldershot. After an eight-week very uncomfortable voyage to India, we spent six months at a cadet college at Bangalore, before being commissioned in September 1941. Thanks to "Boomer" Barrett's influence I was accepted into the Baluchis.

In 1941 the old Imperial Indian Army was going through an enormous and, with hindsight, somewhat imprudent expansion. Regiments which in 1939 consisted of five regular battalions were doubling (and then, after Japan entered the war, redoubling). Pre-war regular battalions were heavily milked of experienced VCOs (Viceroy's Commissioned Officers), Non-Commissioned Officers (NCOs) and senior sepoys; then as soon as newly raised battalions were knitting together they too were milked to meet the demands of the new wave of expansion, and to replace casualties from the heavy fighting in East Africa and the Western Desert.

Whereas in the British Army the core of the foundation of a fighting unit was among the men of the Warrant Officers' and Sergeants' Mess, in the Indian Army a similarly vital role was played by the Viceroy's Commissioned Officers, men who had progressed through the ranks of sepoy, naik (corporal), havildar (sergeant) until they were promoted to be a Viceroy's Commissioned Officer and as a Jemadar took command of a platoon or equivalent sub-unit. Subsequent promotion was to Subedar (probably as a company second-in-command) and finally to Subedar Major, the commanding officer's right-hand man and adviser on a whole range of matters – religion, promotions and opinion throughout the battalion – everything concerned with the attitudes and responses of the Indian soldiers; this was a prestigious post, far more important even than the Regimental Sergeant Major of a British battalion. The entire corps of VCOs was a superb body of men, intelligent, well-educated in military terms, resourceful and utterly loyal, often with extensive active service experience in that demanding testing ground, the North-West Frontier.

Every cavalry and infantry regiment in the Indian Army was allotted what was called "Class Composition" which designated from which of the many martial races of Imperial India the regiment was permitted to recruit. The 10th Baluch Regiment recruited half its men from amongst Punjabi Mussulmans (PMs), in our case from the northern part of the Punjab; a quarter from Pathan tribesmen of the North-West Frontier – Khattaks from around Kohat and Yusufzais to the east of the Khyber Pass around Mardan; and Dogra Brahmins (high caste Hindus) from the Kangra Valley in the Himalayan foothills (see Map Six, p 130). In the 7th Battalion B and D Companies were PMs, A Company Pathans and C Company Dogra Brahmins, with similar proportions among the Signals, Medium Machine Gun, Mortar platoons, drivers and administrative personnel in Headquarter Company.

An Indian battalion only had an establishment of about twelve British officers – Commanding officer (CO), Second in Command (2IC), Adjutant, Quartermaster (QM), four rifle company commanders, Signals Officer (RSO), Motor Transport Officer (MTO) and a couple of Company officers in the Rifle Companies, plus an IMS (Indian Medical Service) Medical Officer (RMO).

On 20 September 1941 Second Lieutenants Charles Coubrough, Dan Pettigrew and John Randle reported to the 7th Battalion 10th Baluch Regiment at Madras. Charles and Dan had been in the same company at Bangalore (and cordially disliked each other), but I had been in a different company and did not know either of them. Dan was sent off almost immediately to be a Liaison Officer at Brigade HQ (after a brief return in 1942, he went sick and never returned). Charles and I got on well and became friends, a friendship which has lasted over sixty years. Our spell at Bangalore had not really trained us for modern all-arms warfare, our knowledge of Urdu, the lingua franca of the Indian Army, was rudimentary and our average age was 19. All we had to offer was youth, the not altogether useless experience of having been through the mill of the British public school system and unbounded enthusiasm.

As a bright-looking chap, Charles was appointed to be Signals Officer, but I was sent off as Company Officer to B Company under an older and very soldierly captain, Dick Gillett. A Company Officer was a somewhat ill-defined post, common only to the Indian Army, with no specific command function, but employed as a general factotum. In practice, when the Company Commander was away, the Company Officer took command, even though technically the Subedar 2IC should have. In November Dick Gillett was posted away to a newly raised parachute battalion and I, having just celebrated my twentieth birthday, found myself in command of a company of a hundred and twenty Punjabi Mussulmans, men of that great warrior race of Northern India. Another equally green Second Lieutenant, Bill Greenwood, was posted as my Company Officer.

I suppose that I might just have made a reasonable section commander; I would have been a pretty raw platoon commander; as a company commander I was quite out of my depth – learning fast, but prone to mistakes of every sort. It speaks volumes for the great spirit and loyalty of the Indian Army, and above all for the trust of the Indian sepoy in his British officers, that he was prepared to serve so well and so loyally, against first class opposition and not just tribesmen, under such raw officers.

GLOSSARY

Basha	Wooden hut made from bamboo and roofed with jungle foliage
Bhisti	Water carrier
Bhutti	Lamp
Bearer	Personal servant or club drink steward
B Echelon	Administrative element of Battalion (Quartermaster/Transport), in rear area during fighting
Chae	Brewed tea
Chapli	Open-toed sandal worn by Frontier tribesmen
Charpoy	Rough string bed
Chowkidar	Watchman
Dhobi	Laundryman
Faqir	Mystic or religious ascetic, usually Muslim
Godown	Warehouse
GSO	General Staff Officer
ICS	Indian Civil Service
IOM	Indian Order of Merit
Jheel	Reservoir
Kote	Armoury
LOB	Left out of Battle
Mali	Gardener

Masalchi	House table servant/club or mess table steward
PIAT	Projectile Infantry Anti-Tank
PM	Punjabi Mussulman
Sweeper	Sanitary man
Taklif	Urdu: personal trouble or grief
Tamasha	Urdu: show, formal party
Tonga	Horse or pony trap
VCO	Viceroy's Commissioned Officer

ILLUSTRATIONS

1. The Author in 1943.

2. Subedar Lal Khan.

3. 7th Battalion, 10th Baluch Regiment Officers and VCOs, Ahmadnagar, October 1941.

4. Charles Coubrough, Ahmadnagar, October 1941.

5. Naik Amir Khan.

6. The Retreat from Burma, 1942. George Holden, the Author, Bill Greenwood and Pat Lindsay.

7. The Retreat from Burma, 1942. Sepoy Allah Dad, the Author, Dan Pettigrew, Siri.

8. Pat Lindsay, 1942.

9. Jock Price, Denys Andrews, "Fish" Herring, Clifford Martin, Shillong, October 1943.

10. Tommy Bruin.

11. Just after the capture of Pegu, May 1945. "Dodgy" Sam Dutt, "Eno" Singha, Author, Joe Hudson, "Dizzy" King, Roderick Maclean, Siri, Clifford Martin, Jock Price.

12. "The Baron" and Norrie Waddell, Kyaikto, September 1945.

13. The Author, Jimmy Whelan, Jock Price, Tony Davies, Kyaikto, February 1946.

14. Clifford Martin, the Author, Subedar Lal Khan, 1976.

15. The Author and Subedar Moghal Baz, 1976.

16. Siri, Pat Dunn, Clifford Martin, 1976.

17. Allan Rowley, the Author, Mike Farrant, Clifford Martin, Charles Coubrough, Ronnie Corson, Tommy Bruin, 2001.

MAPS

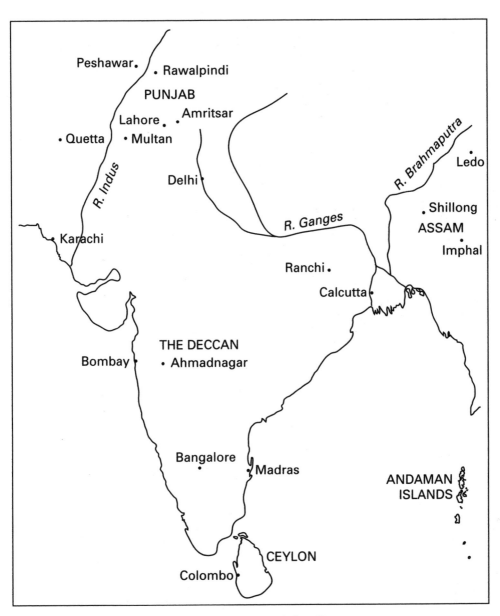

Map One – **Imperial India**

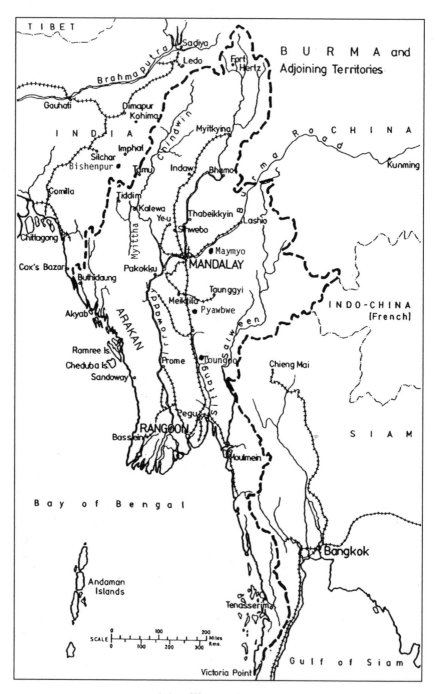

Map Two – **Burma**
(Reproduced with the kind permission of the Burma Campaign
Fellowship Group)

Chapter One

Christmas Leave – Bombay 1941

In the closing months of 1941 the principal non-military pre-occupation of Charles Coubrough and myself was somehow or other to contrive to get leave to go to Bombay over Christmas, a not unusual ambition of two young men to seek the bright lights in wartime.

Throughout this period our newly formed Division, comprised entirely of newly raised wartime Indian battalions, was training in the Deccan in Central India with a view, in the New Year of 1942, to moving to the Middle East, somewhere in Palestine, Syria, Iraq or Iran, in order to relieve a more experienced division already there to go to the Western Desert. All our organization, training and transportation scales were designed for a war in open desert country. With the Japanese not yet in the war, this would be against Germans or Italians either in the Western Desert, along the southern frontier of Turkey or in Iran, if the anticipated German offensive of 1942 into Russia proved to be successful. Because of our impending departure and then later the advent of the war against Japan there was considerable doubt as to whether Lieutenant Colonel Jerry Dyer, our Commanding Officer, would allow any leave at Christmas for the twelve British officers in our battalion.

The culmination of this intensive training was a large divisional exercise in which our brigade was pitted against one of the other brigades, supervised by the divisional staff. I was just 20 and had only been commissioned three months, but such was the rate of the expansion of the Indian Army and the shortage of young officers that I had been appointed the permanent Company Commander of a company of some one hundred and twenty Punjabi Mussulmans. Although I had learnt a great deal during this training period, this was to be my first experience of command in a large exercise. In the final attack my battalion was on the left and was ordered to attack with two companies in the assault. As the most junior and inexperienced company commander, I was most surprised to be given the left forward assault role. I was even more surprised – and disconcerted – to hear that we were to form up just in front of a prominent hill, with an assault of about five or six hundred yards through tall maize on to an enemy position on a small hill on the far side. The battalion plan was somewhat stereotyped (two companies straight up the middle), so I had no option but to follow a similar pattern, with two platoons up, company headquarters just behind on the boundary between the two platoons, and the third platoon in reserve in rear. My left forward platoon (10 Platoon) was commanded on this occasion by the Company Havildar Major, Lal Khan, a huge Punjabi and one of the nicest men I have ever met – loyal, cheerful and willing but not over-burdened with brains. He also had the loudest and most prolonged belch of any man I have ever met, no involuntary burp, hastily stifled by a hand, but a long, deliberate, resonant belch rumbling up from his large deep-chested body. Among men who regarded a belch as a measure of appreciation, it was a sound to gladden the heart of any host or cook. He had 11 Platoon on his right and 12 Platoon in rear. As we set out from the forming-up place across the start line I was horrified to see on the hill behind me not only my Commanding Officer but the Brigade Commander and another imposing red-hatted figure who I assumed was the Divisional Commander. 2Lt Randle and B Company were certainly in the goldfish bowl with a vengeance! All went well to start with. Because of the height of the maize we could not be seen, either from the enemy position nor indeed by my seniors and betters in rear, though they could get some idea of our progress by the movement of the maize. However, after we had been going for a while I suddenly realized that there was no sign of 10 Platoon, who must have veered away to the left and lost contact. 11 Platoon was going steadily forward in the right direction. It was much too late to attempt to send a runner to get 10 Platoon back on track, so I had no alternative but to bring up

2

12 Platoon from reserve on to the left of 11 Platoon and continue my advance towards the objective.

I had no umpire with me, but I knew there was an umpire with the "enemy" company, who by now I could see were Sikhs from a Punjab Regiment. I was pretty certain that he would "umpire" me out, having emerged from the maize and going forward over very open ground in a frontal assault. As we cleared the maize I saw that, on the objective, the "enemy" Company Commander, who I assumed to be as young and callow as myself, had seen our frontal attack developing and in a fit of enthusiasm, not matched by tactical sense, was bringing up his reserve platoon to the forward edge of his position, so that we should be engaged by all three of his platoons as we came forward. I reckoned that I was in for a right drubbing. Then to my immense surprise, over the back of the hill, bearing down on the Sikhs who were all looking towards me, came 10 Platoon led by a triumphant Company Havildar Major Lal Khan. This naturally threw the "enemy" company into some disarray, who had to turn back to face this threat. We were then able to race forward and, just short of the objective, the umpire called a halt and awarded the battle to me. Fortunately my Colonel had not listened in to my orders and, back from the "top brass" vantage point, this fair old muddle appeared to him and to everyone else as a superb piece of tactical deception and handling. I later gathered from Captain Hugh Mercer, the Adjutant, that Jerry Dyer was warmly praised by the Divisional Commander for the skill and vigour of his battalion's attack. My platoon commanders and I alone knew the truth.

In our tented mess that evening Charles Coubrough came to me and said, "John, since it now seems that you are the CO's blue-eyed boy, don't you think it would be a good idea to put in our application for Christmas leave now, while all is well?" I, however, had been musing over the matter and was beginning to feel that perhaps it would be more honest if I went to Jerry and told him what had really happened. I discussed this with Charles and a couple of other subaltern friends. They were all adamant. "Don't be a BF, John. You're certain to make a cock-up of something in the near future and so for heaven's sake build up a bit of credit in the bank!" So next morning Charles and I presented ourselves to Hugh Mercer the Adjutant with a formal application requesting Christmas leave.

He took mine with a smile and said, "Making hay while the sun shines, eh John?" Charles and I duly went to Bombay on our Christmas leave and enjoyed every minute of it; in fact Hugh came with us. Lal Khan shortly got well-deserved promotion to Jemadar and went off to command a platoon in D Company, the other Punjabi Mussulman Company.

I never knew whether Colonel Jerry Dyer believed that B Company was really as well handled as it appeared or whether he realized the truth, and being a wise man kept his knowledge to himself.

Thirty-five years later I had the great pleasure of meeting the now Subedar Lal Khan when I was a guest of my old regiment at the Regimental Centre at Abbottabad in the North-West Frontier Province (of Pakistan), whither he had come specially to meet Clifford Martin, another of his Company Commanders, and me. Among a great deal of talk about the "old days", we had a huge laugh about his great "exploit" in the exercise and how I owed my Christmas leave to him. Sadly the famous belch had lost much of its splendour and timbre – sic transit gloria! Lal Khan is now dead, but I do wonder whether in Valhalla or Paradise or wherever old soldiers go, he is there, with the belch restored to the days of its prime. It would be a bit sad otherwise.

(*This tale originally appeared in the Newsletter of the Indian Army Association*).

A. Background Events

December 1941–February 1942

The Japanese entry into the war in December 1941 changed everything. Our half-trained Division, 17th Indian, instead of going westward to Iraq or Paiforce to continue its training on L of C duties there and thus relieving 10th Indian Division for the Desert, about-faced and went east. 44th and 45th Indian Brigades were sent to Singapore, just in time to be involved in the last days of the fighting there and then go into arduous captivity. In January 1942 our 46th Indian Brigade was sent to Rangoon, together with Division HQ. Such is the innocence of youth that we felt disappointed that we were being siphoned off to a military backwater instead of being given an opportunity to fight the Japanese. It was not an attitude of mind that lasted long or that we ever had again. In December Lt Col C.J. Tomkins the CO was taken ill and so the 2IC Major C.J. (Jerry) Dyer took over command, with Major Pat Dunn as 2IC.

Soon after we docked at Rangoon the GSO1 (Training) of Burma Command came aboard and was talking to Jerry. I heard the latter ask about training areas. "Oh," said the GSO1, "you can't do much training here, its all bloody jungle!!".

In January 1942 the Japanese onslaught on Burma began. One of their expected routes of advance lay across the Salween (that large, mysterious and least known of all the great rivers of Southern Asia) and into southern Burma. After landing in Rangoon in mid-January and being deployed in the Martaban area at the mouth of the river, the battalion was ordered, in mid-February, to take over from 1st/7th Gurkhas further north on the river. Our task was to deny that route by holding the West Bank at the village of Kuzeik opposite the small

5

township of Pa-an at a crossing point, and, by patrolling, to identify any crossings by the enemy, either to the north or to the south, so that the brigade reserve battalion could be brought up to counter-attack and drive the enemy into the river. The river was about as wide as the Rhine at Cologne and imposed a considerable barrier. To start with, my company, B Company, was deployed to hold the actual crossing; A Company (Captain Bill Cayley) and C Company (Captain Siri Kanth Korla) formed patrol bases south and north respectively of the battalion position, whilst D Company (Second Lieutenant Jake Jervis) prepared defences on the western side of our position just in case the Japanese were able to cross and attack us from the rear, before the Brigade counter-attack could be mounted.

Chapter 2

You Just Never Know

It is generally accepted that one of the principal preoccupations of men about to go into battle for the first time is how they are likely to perform in what, rightly or wrongly, is still regarded as one of the more searching tests of a man's worth. Those in command of men, be they Army commanders, commanding tens of thousands, or the humble Section commander with his nine or ten men, are also likely to be giving thought to the likely performance of their subordinates. The more percipient of men will even ponder on how their immediate superior, in the chain of command, will react to the challenge of battle. This story concerns the second of these eternal enigmas.

The command structure of B Company comprised my company Second-in-Command, Subedar Mehr Khan, a tough, grizzled, dour man with much Frontier experience, who, though loyal, was obviously none too happy about being commanded by a boy and who could perhaps have been a little more helpful. 10 Platoon was commanded by Havildar Sabr Hussain, a sound, pleasant self-effacing but not very experienced man; 12 Platoon by Havildar Taja Khan, an interesting man. He was fairly rough and ready, perhaps of not such good stock as the others, and disfigured, as many were in those days, by pockmarks. He had a disconcerting way of hardly ever looking one in the eye, but just occasionally when perhaps it really mattered, he did. He had been a bit of a rogue as a young soldier and knew every trick in the book, but he had a very firm grip on his platoon and was, all in all, a very tough, unflappable chap. Company Headquarters was run by a newly appointed Company Havildar Major (CHM) (equivalent to a Company Sergeant Major in the British Army) Ali Haider Khan, a huge man about six foot three tall, very tough, loyal, cheerful and willing, if not very experienced. Finally there was 11 Platoon Commander Jemadar Bazar Khan, the central figure of this tale. He had been posted to me shortly after I took over command of the company (deliberately, I discovered later, as support for a raw young officer) and was the "beau ideal" of a Jemadar platoon commander, tall, lean, tough, well-educated, willing, loyal, cheerful, helpful in every aspect one could think of. He once had been an Officers' Mess Havildar and had one or two words of English. He also had just the right touch for a young officer, he would be friendly and pull one's leg, but never exceeded that boundary into familiarity. In all our training exercises he was superb – tactically sound, indefatigable, ever cheerful. He was generally regarded as the best platoon commander in the battalion and one much envied by the other rifle company commanders.

For five days things were fairly quiet – some desultory mortar fire from across the Salween and the occasional dive bombing attack, neither of which were particularly effective. The time came for a switch-over with A Company, holding the patrol base some five miles to the south; D Company were to carry out a similar switch with C Company to the north. The orders for the switch were somewhat complicated to disguise the change-over from the Japanese and to maintain a continuous patrol coverage from the patrol bases. At last light, about 6 pm, I was to send off one platoon under my Company 2IC southward; on their arrival at the A Company patrol base, A Company Commander and two of his platoons would set off back to the battalion position, leaving his third platoon under the temporary command of my 2IC. Meanwhile at about the same estimated time, about 8.30 pm, I was to set out with my Company Headquarters and two other platoons; on arrival at the patrol base the third platoon of A Company would rejoin its company in the battalion position. There was one significant omission from the orders, one which I was too green to spot at the time – the laying down of separate routes for A Company's move back and my Company's move south, so that we did not run into each other in the dark. During this change-over the river front facing the Japanese was to be held by the Machine

8

Gun Platoon. Bill Greenwood, my Company Officer, was ordered to stay behind to help A Company settle in.

All started off well. Subedar Mehr Khan and 10 Platoon went off on time, followed at 8.30 pm by me and the rest of the company, 11 Platoon under Bazar Khan leading, followed by Company Headquarters, then 12 Platoon. It was a beautiful, tropical night, full, bright moonlight giving good visibility, yet cool, and we made good progress for about three miles. The track led through secondary jungle and a belt of small holdings where Burmese grew plantains, the local banana, and bamboos; on our left, about twenty yards away, flowed the mighty Salween, while on the right there were occasional stretches of open paddy fields. The one disconcerting feature was that our passage was accompanied by the tapping of bamboo which gave off a somewhat eerie note and appeared to be a signal of some kind. We stopped twice and searched the immediate area to try and identify the source, whereupon it ceased. Suddenly there was a burst of tommy gun fire from the leading 11 Platoon section and one or two rifle shots, and a man came charging down the track, barged into me and disappeared down the way we had come. At first I thought it was one of my own men or that we had blundered into A Company, but then realized it was a Jap. Moving forward, I came across the 11 Platoon section spread across the track looking watchfully ahead. On the track searching a dead Jap for documents was Naik Amir Khan, a cheerful rascally NCO from the Mianwali area of the Punjab, who was an acknowledged expert with the tommy gun.

I ordered a continuation of our march and almost immediately we encountered more Japs in some numbers. Just off the track on the right there was an open stretch of paddy fields across which we saw clearly in the moonlight about thirty Japs and gave them some useful fire with a couple of LMGS. They did not charge, but disappeared into the night. Then away to the south we heard a tremendous fusillade of firing, intensive rifle fire and automatic weapons. This went on for several minutes and then stopped. Clearly Mehr Khan, 10 Platoon and the A Company Platoon were in close contact with the enemy (in fact, though I did not know it at the time, they were overrun by two companies of Japs and virtually wiped out). It seemed to me that there were quite a large number of Japs on our side of the Salween, far more than a mere patrol, and that I should alert Battalion Headquarters. Though we carried a radio even in those days, they were of elementary design and at night "mush" descended and any sort of communication, voice or morse, became virtually impossible and this sadly proved to be the case now. The only alternative was to fall back on the age-old messenger on foot. I wrote a brief report on a message pad and gave it to Sepoy Nasir Mohammed, the company bugler and runner, to take back the way we had come, to Battalion Headquarters. He set off, but had barely gone two hundred yards when we heard terrible screams from him and cries of "Bas, bas" (Enough, enough). Clearly the Japs had moved in behind us and were astride the track back to Battalion Headquarters.

With Japanese in some strength ahead of us, behind us and to the right, and the Salween on our left, it seemed to me that I had a problem on my hands. I therefore decided to summon the two platoon commanders and the Company Havildar Major to review the situation and issue fresh orders. We gathered in the moonlight and I remember thinking that the situation was pretty hairy, that I was going to need some good support, and, thank God, that I had such a stalwart platoon commander as Bazar Khan.

As we assembled, at that moment, of all moments, Bazar Khan cracked; "crack" is really the wrong word; it was a chasm. He stood there, tears in his eyes, wringing his hands and sobbing, "Sahib, we are finished, we are surrounded". To say that I was amazed is a serious understatement; nothing in my whole life before or since has ever come quite as such an utter and unnerving surprise. Here was the crack platoon commander of the Battalion, the "beau sabreur", the experienced soldier, unmanned and sobbing like some child, just when those qualities were so desperately needed. Nothing in my limited military experience, School Officers' Training Corps, the Officers' School at Bangalore, the books that I had read, had any bearing. The one thing that crack platoon commanders did not do was to crack! All sorts of wild ideas and possible courses of action flashed through my mind; threatening him with my revolver (too melodramatic even for that situation and not likely to help); haranguing him into regaining his manhood (my Urdu wasn't up to it and it would take too long); putting him under arrest and getting his platoon havildar to take over (my knowledge of the legal niceties of putting an officer under arrest was sketchy) – all this churned around madly in my mind. In the event I did the right thing for the wrong reasons – I simply ignored him – and then did the wrong thing for the right reasons by temporarily taking over direct command not only of his three sections but those of 12 Platoon. I called out in the dark to each section commander by name, ordering them in turn to take up a sort of laager position so that we were in a circle, each section linking up with the others. All this time Havildar Taja Khan of 12 Platoon, to his eternal credit, stood there impassively. He made no protest at my assuming, albeit temporarily, command of his platoon. All this section readjustment took a little time. Then another party of Japs was spotted and engaged with our Brens and so I dismissed the two Platoon Commanders back to their platoons, Bazar Khan having somehow regained his composure. Although he was very subdued, I just had to hope that he would be capable of adequate command for the remainder of that night.

The rest of the events of that busy night have no bearing on this story; somehow I was able to get back to the main Battalion position with only a few casualties, and probably the Japs were, in fact, as confused as we were. (Long after the war we learnt that the whole of a battalion of the crack Japanese 33rd Division had crossed that night.) I pondered hard as to whether to tell Jerry Dyer about Bazar Khan's failure and decided that, at the moment, he had enough worries. It ceased to matter; soon after getting back to the Battalion position, it was dive-bombed for four hours by relays of bombers from Chieng Mai, across the border in Siam; the next night the entire battalion position was attacked and overrun by two battalions of Japs (See B – Background Events). I never really found out how Bazar Khan died. 11 Platoon stood their ground and fought well, so I like to believe that he redeemed himself and died like a soldier. The point of this story is, I hope, made. Here was a man whom everyone, an experienced commanding officer, all the other officers, the Subedar Major and I, were certain was a born leader and man of action. Yet when it came to the test he failed, at a critical moment, to meet the challenge. You just never know until the moment comes.

B. Background Events

February–September 1942

On the night of 11/12 February 1942 two battalions of 215 Regiment of the crack 33rd Japanese Division attacked and, after several hours of fighting, overran the Battalion. My B Company, consisting of Company HQ, a Section of Vickers Medium Machine Guns and 11 Platoon, was required to hold a three-platoon front (10 Platoon had been wiped out the night before and Colonel Jerry Dyer required 12 Platoon to go out on a battalion patrol just before the battle). We gave a good account of ourselves and killed a number of Japs, but were eventually overrun. Bill Greenwood and I and two other sepoys from B Company, Pat Dunn (2IC), Siri and George Holden (Machine Gun Officer) and a few VCOs and men (including 12 Platoon) were all able to break out, although it took me two days to get back to British lines. Colonel Jerry Dyer and 288 VCOs and men were killed, and 229, including Bill Cayley, Hugh Mercer (Adjutant), 'Toots' Toothill (Quartermaster), Jake Jervis and the Regimental Medical Officer were taken prisoner. Charles Coubrough, the Signals Officer, after a determined and indeed valiant attempt to escape, was only captured two days later twenty miles from Kuzeik and nearly in safety. All our wounded, including Jerry Dyer (but sparing 'Toots'), were butchered by the Japanese, an atrocity which governed the Battalion's attitude then and for the rest of the war. Siri, who alone of the companies, had all his platoons present, put up a fine show and was awarded an immediate DSO. Naik Amir Khan of my 11 Platoon won a posthumous IOM (Indian Order of Merit), roughly equivalent to the Distinguished Conduct Medal. This epic battle is generally referred to as the Battle of Pa-an or the Battle of Kuzeik–Pa-an. I use the former.

The remnants reassembled at a township called Thaton under Pat

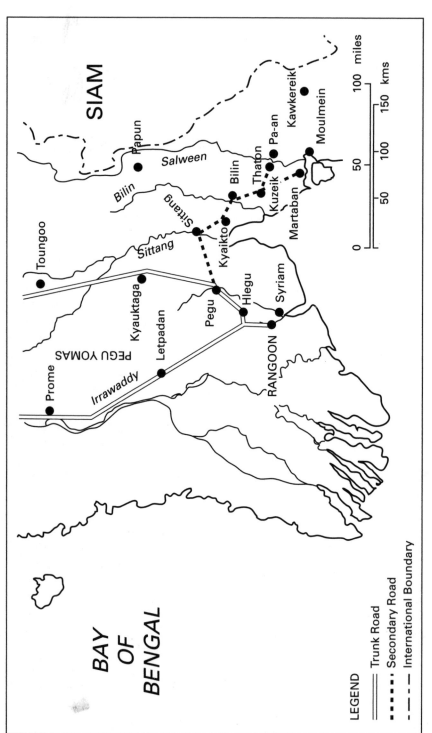

Map Three – **Southern Burma**

LEGEND
Trunk Road
Secondary Road
International Boundary

Dunn, and I took over command of a weak composite company containing all the Punjabi Mussulman survivors of B and D Companies.

A week later we were involved in the Sittang River Bridge debacle when the only bridge over that river was prematurely blown, leaving most of our Division on the wrong side. The marching element of the Battalion was fortunately sent across before the bridge was blown, but we lost our MTO Tony Turner, who had been LOB (left out of battle) at Pa-an, and about another 100 men, mostly drivers and administrative staff; so we had lost eight out of our thirteen officers and over 600 VCOs and men in just a week. Dan Pettigrew and Roderick Maclean, who had been Brigade Liaison and Brigade Orderly Officers respectively, joined us when 46 Brigade was disbanded, following the virtual destruction of all its three battalions. Despite this appalling loss the Battalion maintained its cohesion, first under Pat Dunn, then, after he was injured, by Siri.

After the Fall of Rangoon I developed a serious infection in my leg and was evacuated by hospital paddle steamer to Mandalay and then to the hill station of Maymyo. Fortunately there my leg healed quickly and I was able to rejoin the Battalion. Meanwhile Colonel Pat Lindsay had been flown in to take over command and Siri had reverted to 2IC and C Company Commander (Dogras). On my return, as my old Company was now commanded by George Holden, I took over C Company from Siri and commanded them for the long and arduous march out of Burma. Dogras were delightful soldiers to command, courteous, well-disciplined and tough. We eventually reach Imphal in early May just as the monsoon broke. A new 2IC, Major George Tarver, appeared, Siri took over his old company and I was made Adjutant. After several months hanging about in the North Assam frontier area near Ledo we moved to Ranchi in Eastern India for leave, reinforcement and retraining.

Chapter 3

Loot

Looting is not an activity to which the British Army has contributed a great deal of literature, history or data, except that it is rigorously forbidden. Doubtless in earlier times British soldiers, following the custom of the time, sacked and pillaged captured cities, and there have, inevitably, in the two World Wars, been cases of looting by individuals or indisciplined bodies of troops. Certainly large quantities of livestock, especially poultry, goats, eggs and fruit were "liberated" in Burma in the Second World War, but the looting of other personal property and valuables was not widespread and, if discovered, was dealt with severely. This is a tale about an apparent contradiction in terms – official looting.

In March 1942 the British forces in Burma, having suffered heavily at the Sittang River débâcle, were falling back towards Rangoon and, though we in my battalion did not know it, the decision had already been taken to give up that city without a serious defence and retreat northwards, eventually into India. The remnants of the battalion were holding a series of important bridges some forty miles north-east of Rangoon, my much depleted company on one of them, when Pat Dunn, the acting Commanding Officer, sent for me. He told me that Rangoon was not to be defended and that therefore authority had been given for each unit to send one officer, with a small fatigue party and a three-ton truck, to take what they could find in Rangoon which would be of welfare value to their men. He gave me an official pass authorizing me to do this, suggesting that I went for fags, tea, sugar and condensed milk for the "chae" so beloved by Indian soldiers, not forgetting a bit of the hard stuff for the six surviving officers in the Battalion. Taking a couple of sepoys from my company, I set out in a three-tonner for Rangoon.

Compared to many cities in the East, Rangoon at that time was not only fairly large and modern but well-spaced-out, with many wide avenues. The Japanese had bombed it frequently since early January and I knew that most of the population had fled. However, doubtless because they anticipated capturing it soon, the Japanese had recently held off their bombing and I assumed that many civilians would have returned. To my considerable surprise this was not so, and mile after mile of fine broad streets were completely empty. Burmah Oil Company personnel, assisted by our sappers, had been given the job of destroying the large oil refinery at Syriam, just outside the city across the Rangoon River, and an enormous pall of black smoke covered half of the sky. This ominous overcast sky and the miles of completely empty streets produced a chilling aura of defeat. I met no civilians at all; there were one or two other officers on a similar errand to my own with whom I exchanged information. Some military police, "Red Caps", stopped me, checked my credentials and waved me on. Down in the docks a party of Royal Marines was heaving cases of whisky into the water: "Not going to let those buggers (the Japanese) get this lot!"

I managed to fill the three-tonner with the requisite fags, tea, etc, and some hard stuff for my brother officers, and I was about to set out back when I remembered the Army and Navy Stores. Out of idle curiosity I took my truck there, expecting to find it either locked and bolted or ransacked, but it was neither. The doors were unlocked and there was this large emporium with all its goods displayed just for the taking. I suddenly realized with an awful primeval thrill that I could simply help myself from this treasure trove, the only problem being that my truck was already bulging. I wasn't really very clever. I got some books for my brother officers to read: I clearly remember that one of them was Freud's *Anatomy of Sex*, whose case histories made fascinating reading for a lot of sex-starved young officers as it was passed around. For some extraordinary reason which I simply cannot explain even now, the only other loot I can recall taking was a set of golf clubs. It was quite ridiculous, as the chances of playing any game, let alone golf, in the immediate future were negligible.

17

I set off back to the Battalion where my loot was received with approbation, except for some derisive remarks about the golf clubs, which were in any case "bagged" by Battalion Headquarters.

Someone distributed the clubs among Battalion Headquarters and, whenever my company was anywhere near them on the march out, I could not but smile at seeing these clubs, including the woods, being used as walking sticks by the Battalion headquarter's personnel. We eventually reached India and safety and, six weeks later, I was made Adjutant. Shortly after my taking over, Pat Lindsay said, "By the way, John, how about getting all those golf clubs in, as they might be useful when some of us go on leave?" I duly did so and all were recovered except a number four or five iron, admittedly the worse for wear. I informed Pat who put on a magnificent display of mock anger about the missing club. "Put the chap on a charge and I'll teach him to lose valuable golf clubs." Just for a moment I thought he was being serious.

Years later in England I met a very senior man in the Army and Navy Stores organization at a party and told him this story, thinking that he would be amused. On the contrary, he was clearly quite put out and seemed to regard me as some sort of criminal. I even had the feeling that he would have liked to have invoiced me for the golf clubs.

Chapter 4

The Luck Of The Irish

Stories of miraculous escapes from death or capture in war are fairly commonplace. I cannot pretend that this true story of such an escape is particularly exceptional, but, if nothing else, it illustrates most vividly the well-known luck of the Irish.

The retreat of the British Army from Burma in the early part of 1942 is generally reckoned to have been one of the longest and most arduous ever endured by a British or Imperial Army. It was certainly a severe testing ground for all the military virtues of endurance, discipline and leadership. It was only possible because of the miracles of improvisation carried out by the administrative staff of Army Headquarters there, under the direction of Generals Alexander and Slim. Though General Slim pays tribute to this in his book *Defeat Into Victory*, it is not generally realized what a superb job they did. Though we were often short of food and water, or at least of drinkable water (Burma was not short of water, but with cholera rife much of it was heavily contaminated), in my experience this never became critical nor indeed were we ever short of ammunition or petrol, the other sinews of war.

One of the main problems of a prolonged series of forced marches is that fatigue becomes cumulative. After a while all one's thoughts, apart from carrying out one's military duties, become obsessed by the imperative desire to go to sleep, and stay asleep. Having been brought up on P.C. Wren's stories of Beau Geste, with the attributed motto of the French Foreign Legion, "March or die", I came to realize that that cliché had much truth in it.

Battalions of our division were ordered in turn to form the

rearguard and it fell to my lot on two occasions, as a Company Commander, to be the rearguard commander. By day this not only involved keeping a wary eye out for any following Japanese but also rounding up stragglers who had fallen by the way. This added to our fatigue, because in so doing the rearguard company tended to fall behind the main column. Getting utterly exhausted men on their feet and marching was a difficult job. Some responded to exhortations, but in the last resort it was often a question of prodding or even kicking a man to his feet to get him moving. On one occasion I had the unedifying duty of having to harangue the Machine Gun Officer of a distinguished British Regiment in front of my own company of Indian soldiers, a task I found distinctively distasteful. Some men, and even officers, simply gave up the ghost. One portly Staff Officer simply sat down and told me, "I'd rather die, than march any more," and die in due course he did, I subsequently heard. By night this shepherding was generally not possible unless one found a man actually on the track. Sleep and overcoming it became the predominant factor; all anyone wanted to do was just to sink down wherever one could and go to sleep; even the traditional fakir's bed of nails seemed a delightful prospect.

On the second occasion, because it was night I, as the Company Commander, had the traditional honour, so they said, of being the last man in the company and indeed the very last man of the formed British Army retreating out of Burma. It was an anxious task and I have to admit to quite often looking back over my shoulder, particularly as, being in brilliant tropical moonlight, one could see for some distance, always wondering whether we would see the glint of Japanese bayonets and hear the cry of "Banzai". My imagination was over-fanciful; nothing, in fact, happened and we were to learn long afterwards that the Japanese at that particular stage were not following up very hard.

One of the minor phenomena of war is the way in which one is often thrown together with a complete stranger and for a few minutes or hours finds oneself in the close company of a man one has never met before and very often never meets again. It is another paradox of war how this establishes a close bond at the time, in a way which seldom occurs in casual meetings in peacetime. My companion for that night's rearguard march was an Indian medical officer, a captain and of that very well known Indian family of Tata who were then probably the biggest industrial and commercial private empire in the whole of India. Why a doctor was ordered to be with me I never discovered. He admittedly carried a haversack with some medical supplies, but there was very little that he could do. He was a delightful man and I have often wished that I could have met him again in a more relaxed situation. I cannot pretend that the circumstances were ideal for a stimulating conversazione, but he was certainly extremely good company, with a fund of amusing stories which helped to pass the time and fight off the inevitable danger of relaxing one's alertness. Because of the danger of men going to sleep and failing to get up after a halt, I had to establish a very strict drill after every stop. Each section commander was ordered on the fall-in after a halt physically to go up and touch every man of his section on the shoulder checking their names and then to report to the platoon commander who would then, together with a man from Company Headquarters, send a runner to me personally to report that their platoon and company headquarters men were on their feet and ready to march.

On this occasion we had been marching for thirty-six hours with only brief halts for rest and food – certainly no sleep – and were all very tired. Inevitably, at one halt the worst happened and a section commander, either due to carelessness or his own fatigue, failed to carry out an adequate check and one sepoy, Girdhari Lal, who had been Pat Dunn's orderly, was left behind. I could have forgiven this, but what really annoyed me was that either because he did not know or through lack of a sense of duty, the section commander failed to report it until much later.

Shortly after dawn we reached a small Burmese town where, to our great joy, we were told that we could have an hour's rest and there would be motor transport to ferry the Battalion on for some miles. I was however, very concerned about Girdhari Lal and, though we only had about three vehicles in the Battalion, I asked Pat Lindsay to let me take one. It was of course loaded to the gunwales with battalion kit, but I wanted to drive back down the way we had come to see if I could find Girdhari Lal. Pat agreed and said that, if the Battalion moved off before I returned, he would leave a messenger at an agreed place in the town from whom I could pick up instructions as to where to rejoin the Battalion. I therefore set off with a couple of sepoys as escort somewhat apprehensively down the way we had come, hoping, that I would not run into any Japanese.

The problem as I saw it was that Girdhari Lal might well have slipped a few yards off the track into some cover, might still be fast asleep, and so not see or hear us on our way back. Accordingly, we went slowly back down the track halting every few hundred yards to sound the horn and shout, but there was no sign of him. We had gone back about as far as I deemed it prudent to go when one of the sepoys sitting on the kit on the top of the truck shouted that there was a figure about three-quarters of a mile ahead of us. Delighted with this news, we drove down there quickly, only to find, to my disappointment, that it was not Girdhari Lal but a British soldier, in the last stages of exhaustion, stumbling along only half conscious with fatigue and thirst. He turned out to be from the Royal Inniskilling Fusiliers and was overjoyed to see us. We hauled him into the back of the truck and then sadly turned back to rejoin the Battalion, also picking up on the way a very badly wounded Chinese soldier of the Ninth Chinese Route Army who had got lost. We met a Chinese jeep on the road and handed him over.

I eventually caught up with the Battalion and, handed the fusilier over to Battalion Headquarters, who assured me that they would see him on his way to rejoin his own battalion. I had to report that I had not found Girdhari Lal, about which I was very depressed, but I felt that I had done all I could.

There was a happy sequel. About a week later the battalion was holding positions on a tributary of the Chindwin River, forming a lay-back position through which other units of the division were retreating. There were crowds of Indian civilian refugees passing, men, women and children, many in the last stages of exhaustion, many dying of cholera near our position. Suddenly Girdhari Lal appeared, dirty and dishevelled, grinning all over his face and still carrying his rifle. I was delighted to see him, to hear his astonishing story of escape and to congratulate him on his efforts. My Subedar, Sohan Lal, a grizzled professional veteran of much fighting on the Frontier, was not impressed. He came to me and said, "Sahib, I think we shall have to put Girdhari Lal on a charge". "Oh come on, Subedar Sahib, I think he has done very well." "It's not the going to sleep on the march, Sahib, that I'm concerned about, but his rifle is absolutely filthy, the barrel is dirty and he clearly hasn't cleaned it for over a week!" It was not often that I disregarded the advice of Sohan Lal.

I sometimes wonder what happened to the Inniskilling Fusilier and whether he survived the war. I like to think that somewhere in Ireland is a grizzled old soldier who, even now, for the umpteenth time, and to their affectionately disguised boredom, is telling his grandchildren or the boys at Murphy's bar over their porter, of his miraculous escape from death or arduous captivity back in the dark days in Burma.

Chapter 5

The Line

One of the characteristics which marked the difference between the generation which fought in the First World War and that which fought in the Second was the reluctance of the former to talk about their experiences. Whether this was due to the fact that in an earlier age men simply did not talk about their exploits in war and maintained the stiff upper lip tradition, or whether, because the experiences of those who fought in the front line in the First World War were so awful, the fact remains that they did not. Certainly, as far as my father and his generation were concerned, they never did talk about it in my presence when I was a boy.

There was one exception to this. One winter's day, when I was very young, my parents had given a lunch party which went on until into the early evening. My father's friends were in the drawing room, whilst the ladies and my younger brother were elsewhere. When it got dark and the curtains were drawn, they sat there in the firelight and, for once, started talking about the Great War. I was sitting on the floor beside my father's chair, in the shadows, and after a while they clearly forgot my presence as the whisky decanter circulated. Every now and again, as they talked, the expression "the Line" or "going up the Line" recurred. I was fascinated by this, as I simply could not understand what the line was they were talking about. What could this line be? I remember being in an agony of indecision as to whether to give way to my almost unbearable curiosity and ask them, at the risk of being told to leave the room, or simply to sit there in silence and endeavour to find out afterwards. Perhaps prudently, I took the latter course. Eventually, of course, I came to know what the expression meant and in my own turn in the Second World War found myself either in the Line or Moving up the Line or Down the Line, though the nature of the fighting in the Second World War and the general absence of trench warfare robbed the phrase of its true significance.

Years later, after the Second World War, I read a most interesting article by a soldier-writer who moved "up the Line" from the base areas, describing most accurately and evocatively the sequence of units and men that he met as he moved towards the front. He started off in a base area with its vast workshop areas, transport lines, ammunition dumps, ration dumps, petrol dumps and bridging dumps, with the attendant signs of organized military chaos. He described casualty clearing stations, with their steady inflow and outflow of casualties. As he approached the divisional areas, he recorded the changing pattern of noise: the first sound of guns, obviously increasing until he actually saw the gun position of the Heavy and Medium guns; further forward still to the music, as some gunners quaintly describe it, of the Field and Mountain guns, and all the terrible, awesome orchestration of war. He described sapper dumps and Divisional and Brigade Headquarters past the tank laagers of the armoured regiments until he finally reached what he described with some poignancy as the lonely and yet uplifting world of the infantry. Finally he described the different types of men that he met at each step of the progression forward, a little disparagingly of the base and staff officers and men, but with a human and penetrating analysis of the difference. He added the interesting observation, and it has been made by others, that wherever you went during the War, in the Western Desert, Burma, Italy or Normandy, the men you met in the front lines were, if not the same men, all the same sort of men, different from the support and base troops.

He also made much of the paradox of war, its appalling horrors and utter drudgery, and yet just occasionally its stirring majesty and pageantry. No one who has ever seen a Mountain battery going into action for real will ever forget it – magnificent mules and fine strong men.

So too, to see a regiment of tanks, regimental or squadron pennants flying from radio aerials, going into battle quickens the blood. I have often wondered what it must have felt like on British

25

warships in either of the two World Wars just before action to see the battle ensign hoisted, with probably a strange feeling of excitement and fear. But I personally believe that the most splendid and moving sight of all is to see a battalion of infantry moving up. Here there is no machinery, no equipment, just the basic human element of mankind at war, singing, whistling, joking; at other times, when the going is hard, a grey look of fatigue, mixed with a sort of potpourri of fear, of endurance, of determination and of pride, and just occasionally, when coming out of the Line, utter and abject exhaustion and dejection.

Going up the Line had its lighter moments. In early 1943 my battalion was moving from Ranchi in Bihar to Imphal in the battle zone on the Assam/Burma border. The move involved a number of changes from broad- to narrow-gauge railway, from rail to paddle steamer on the Brahmaputra, and finally one hundred and fifty miles by road. Being half mounted infantry, we had several hundred horses and mules and so the move was a long and complex one. It was also a classic example of being messed about by arrogant, unhelpful and incompetent Movement Control Staff. After about a week tempers, not least that of Pat Lindsay, our much liked but irascible Commanding Officer, were decidedly frayed. The Battalion embarked on a paddle steamer on the Brahmaputra for a voyage upstream. After several hours of delay a particularly callow Movement Control Second Lieutenant approached Pat and, without too much respect, announced, "I am appointing you Officer in Charge". To be told by this off-hand puppy that he was appointed to command his Battalion almost reduced Pat to apoplexy.

A further two-hour delay ensued at the end of which Pat announced, "I've had enough of this," and stormed up to the Serang, the Bengali Captain of the boat, and ordered him to cast off and get under way at once. There was some initial protest about the permission of the "Movement Control Sahibs", but this was brushed aside, for, after all, the Serang knew the difference between a Second Lieutenant and a Lieutenant-Colonel commanding a battalion of fighting troops. We had just cast off when the egregious Second Lieutenant came rushing along the jetty, gesticulating and shouting, "Stop, Stop. I haven't authorized you to leave". Pat grimly ordered the Serang to keep going. About half a

26

dozen of our officers, myself included, were on the rear deck, where we had been having lunch, with, on the table, a bunch of un-consumed bananas. I regret to say that we armed ourselves with these bananas and sent a volley of well-directed missiles to straddle the hapless Second Lieutenant. Above the noise of the paddles, moving up to full speed, we could hear a plaintive cry of "You'll hear more of this. I shall report you". Pat Lindsay had not been born the day before and he promptly produced a long catalogue of the incompetence of the Movement Control Staff, which was naturally supported by our Brigade and Divisional Commanders. It did not include any reference to bananas, but it did have the desired effect of improving the lot of subsequent units in coming up the line.

One particular incident of a battalion going up the line is etched forever in my memory. In the earlier part of the retreat from Burma our division was east of the River Sittang in Lower Burma. For the first hundred miles of that not inconsiderable river there was only one crossing, a combined road and rail bridge which very much made it the jugular vein of the Division in its fighting withdrawal. My Battalion, which was two miles east of the bridge, recovering from its severe mauling at Pa-an, was ordered to move along the railway line and to cross over the bridge to the west bank. In so doing we came under quite unexpected enemy fire, unexpected because all information was that the Japanese were miles away. As the leading company commander, I managed to get through to the bridge and, instead of crossing over as originally ordered, felt it right, until my own Acting Commanding Officer Pat Dunn arrived, to report to the Commanding Officer of the bridge guard battalion to see if my company could be of some help. This was readily accepted and I was sent up to reinforce a company of the 12th Frontier Force Regiment which was already coming under attack from Japanese who had come in from the flank and were now attempting to seize the bridge, thereby cutting off the whole division. After a while there was a lull in the fighting and I and my company were able to take some stock of our surroundings. We were on high ground from which to the westward we could see right across the bridge. After more fire, I looked over the bridge and saw, on it, and moving eastward towards our side of the river, a large body of British soldiers. They were men of the Duke of

27

Wellington's Regiment and it was a fine and stirring sight to see such a body of men in all their cheerful, soldierly pride in themselves and in their regiment, moving up the Line. As they cleared the bridge and headed on to join the bridge guard, strangely my mind went back to that time long ago when as a young boy I sat by my father's fireside hearing for the first time about battalions moving up the Line in Flanders.

Pat Dunn and the rest of the Battalion reached the bridgehead and I was ordered to rejoin them and cross over the river westwards to comparative safety on the west bank. During the night, due to intense Japanese pressure, a series of communication failures and the usual fog of war, the bridge was blown, leaving most of the Division on the east or enemy side of the bridge. At dawn I went down with my company to do all I could to help exhausted British, Gurkha and Indian soldiers who had swum across the river under enemy mortar and machine-gun fire as they reached the west bank. Inevitably, among them were men of the Duke's who had been in almost continuous fighting since I had seen them some sixteen hours before. I could not but be shaken by the dramatic change in their appearance and indeed the fortunes of war.

The phrase Going Up The Line is now completely outmoded, a blueprint Dad's Army phrase, but on the rare occasions when I hear it I always recall the Duke's on that far-off day.

C. Background Events

October 1942–March 1944

In October 1942 the Battalion reassembled in Ranchi in Eastern India to receive a massive influx of new officers and men. The officers included several who were to serve with distinction for the rest of the war in the Battalion or until they were killed: Brian Harding (2IC), Clifford Martin (A Company), Denys Andrews (C Company) and Jock Price (Intelligence Officer and later Mortar Officer).

A new type of infantry battalion had been thought up – a Reconnaissance Battalion – for the planned counter-offensive in Burma. In outline it consisted of two companies of infantry mounted on ponies with mule transport in support and two companies of jeep-borne infantry. Battalion HQ and the support platoons were organized to operate with either the mounted infantry or the jeeped infantry in the lead, depending on the tactical situation.

The Battalion therefore had a massive retraining requirement, not only to absorb all the new infantry tactics learnt from the mistakes in the Retreat but a considerable degree of animal management and Motor Transport driving and maintenance skills. A Company became a PM (Punjabi Mussulman) Company, along with D Company. B Company became the Pathan Company and C Company remained the Dogra Brahmin Company.

After three months' initial training in Ranchi in January 1943 the Battalion moved to Imphal, in North-East India where we hoped we could continue our training. This did not prove practical and in April 1943 we moved to Shillong, a hill station in Assam, for a further six months' training. In October 1943 we moved to rejoin 17 Division, who were holding forward positions in the Chin Hills, south of Tiddim on the Indo/Burmese frontier.

Three other officers of note joined us about that time: Tommy Bruin (Company Officer A Company and later IO and Company Commander), Joe Hudson (D Company) and Jimmy Whelan (Mortar Officer and Adjutant).

Chapter 6

"London"

Most people, as they go through life, find that certain words, phrases, sounds, music or scents, which may be unexceptional and commonplace to others, take on a special significance to them, because of some particularly evocative memory from the past. This is a tale of one such everyday word, "London", which always has a special meaning for me and for one other of my comrades-in-arms.

It is also a story of the "special relationship" which existed in the Second World War between the Infantry and the Gunners of the British, and doubtless of every other army. Superficially, there might have appeared to be disharmony. The Infantry pretended to regard the Gunners as being a touch cocky for a mere supporting rather than a fighting arm, with a tendency to adopt, sometimes genuinely and sometimes spuriously, an air of horsiness (*pace* the well-known Infantry officer's translation of the Staff College motto "*Tam marte quam Minerva*" as "Too many Gunners get on my nerves!"). The term 'dropshorts' also featured in conversation.

The Gunners pretended to regard the Infantry as a pedestrian lot, not very good at map-reading and too often dependent on gunner radio communications. On the battlefield all this disappeared and the one thing every experienced Infantry company or battalion commander desired and worked for was to have a really close and mutually reliant trust with his FOO (Forward Observation Officer) or battery commander. "Having your gunner in your pocket" was a buzz-phrase of the Second World War in Burma.

The 25-pounder Territorial Regiment, 129 Field Regiment,

supporting our brigade came from the Edinburgh area. By 1944 they were as fine and professional a body of gunners as any battalion could possibly hope to have in support. Unlike some regular soldiers before the war, the men had joined the Territorial Army as a matter of patriotic duty, not simply to avoid the dole. They were also men in their mid-twenties, not the boy conscripts that so many British units contained at this latish stage in the war. Officers and sepoys alike in my battalion regarded them with the highest respect, both as men and as gunners.

In late 1943 and early 1944 our division was at Tiddim in the Chin Hills on the Indo-Burmese border facing south-eastwards, astride one of the secondary routes between these two countries. The highest point and one which was held by our forces was Kennedy Peak, 8871 feet above sea level. Anything in and around India under ten thousand feet was always regarded as a hill!

My Battalion was on the extreme right and open flank of the Division, with the Manipur River on our right and with our Battalion Headquarters located near a small Chin village called Saizang. We had two forward rifle companies, with the remainder back in Imphal looking after our ponies and mules. The most forward of these two companies, A Company, commanded by Clifford Martin but without the customary gunner FOO, was on a feature, Point 6052, just to the south of a Chin village called Mualbem; B Company was at Vangte. The scenery was magnificent in the cool, clear days of the Indo-Burma cold weather. A vast panorama of scrub-covered hills stretched south and westward, and the huge bulk of Khum Vum, an outcrop of Kennedy Peak, loomed above us to the east. Three thousand feet below us the Manipur River glinted in the sun and in the quiet of the night one could sometimes hear its waters.

The bulk of the divisional artillery, including our supporting Field Regiment, was concentrated on Kennedy Peak, whence they could engage targets on most of the divisional front. Because we were so far away to the right and because of technical crest-clearance problems, our Battalion, most exceptionally, had been allocated a section of two 25 pounders, located inside the Battalions Headquarters perimeter at Saizang and under command of a sergeant. As the crow flew, the distance between Battalion Headquarters and A Company on Point 6052 was thirteen thou-

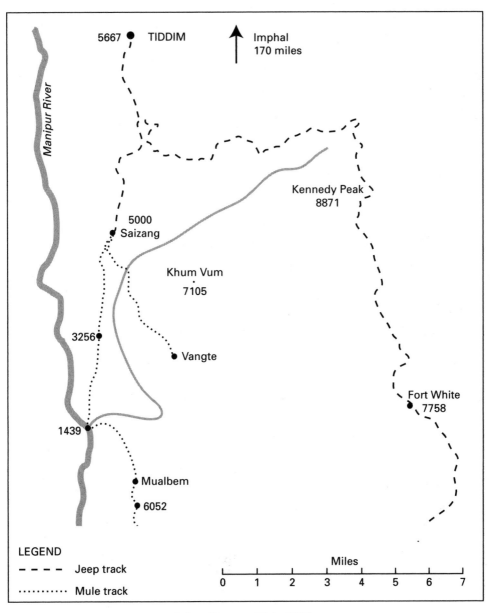

5667 ● TIDDIM

↑ Imphal
170 miles

Manipur River

Kennedy Peak
8871

5000
● Saizang

Khum Vum
·
7105

3256 ●

● Vangte

Fort White
● 7758

1439 ●

● Mualbem

● 6052

LEGEND
– – – Jeep track
·········· Mule track

Miles
0   1   2   3   4   5   6   7

Map Four – Chin Hills

sand yards, just under seven miles, and just within range of Saizang because the altitude gave shells a few extra hundred yards of range. By track the journey took many hours and involved descending from about 5000 feet at Saizang to 1400 feet on the Manipur River and then climbing up again to Point 6052, a fair old slog for men and mules.

There was not much serious fighting to begin with, but a great deal of arduous and sometimes dangerous patrolling. The Japanese had little artillery, but occasionally did a bit of harassing fire with some long-range 105 millimetre or 155 millimetre guns (they interrupted our 1943 Christmas Dinner with some of it).

One of the principal areas of infantry/artillery cooperation was the provision of defensive fire (DF). In every defensive position within range of guns, even for a one-night stand, a company commander would select one or two areas in front of his position which posed the greatest threat; especially covered approaches to our positions or forming-up areas in dead ground, ground which could not be seen and covered by small arms fire. Each of these was worked out by the gunners, usually by silent registration called prediction, but sometimes by actually firing shells to "register" the target. The latter could obviously guarantee the fire exactly where one wanted it, but if enemy patrols had spotted the registration it lost much of its potential effect. The gunners gave each of these mutually agreed targets a code letter and number. For ease of communication, especially in the heat of battle, code names were also agreed, such as a series of football teams, makes of car, cricketers, with place names in Britain being favourites. The important thing was to select names which could not be confused: "Malvern" and "Morden" would not have been sensible! Forward or very exposed companies were, by agreement with the gunners, allowed to designate the most important of these "DF" tasks as a "DF (SOS)" task. This meant that, although guns would often be used for engaging targets on other parts of the front, once that particular task was finished, at least two guns (a section) and usually four guns (a troop) would be permanently laid on that DF (SOS) task, available (together with any other DF task) to be called for by the FOO allotted to a company or, if no FOO was allocated, by the company commander himself. The gunners would then automatically fire a standard number of rounds per gun, which I think was three at that time, on any DF task called for. They would only fire further rounds when called upon to "repeat". It was clearly the job of the company commander, the battle adjutant (or other duty officer at Battalion Headquarters) and the gunner chain of command to be instantly *au fait* with what these code names were. A company on Point 6052 had a number of such DF tasks, with "London" being the DF (SOS) task.

Throughout the war in Burma we always "stood-to" for about an hour, from half an hour before dawn and from half an hour before sunset. The latter was important so that, in the event of the frequent night fighting, everyone knew where he had to be and who was around him. The pre-dawn stand-to was essential because the Japanese frequently attacked around dawn. The period after the morning stand-to was always one of the most pleasant and relaxed of the day, the potential hazards of the night were over, the sun was warming but not oppressive, men sat about cleaning weapons, loading magazines, writing letters, washing and shaving and inevitably drinking mugs of hot sweet tea, "chae" to the Indian soldier, "char" to the British soldier of that era, as "gun fire" was to those of the First World War.

One day in March 1944 we stood down after a dawn stand-to following a quiet night. I had just got back into my bunker to shave when a signaller arrived breathlessly outside, summoning me to the forward radio link in the Battalion Headquarter's bunker to talk urgently to "A Company Commander Sahib". As this was unusual, I went as quickly as I could and called up A Company. Back came Clifford Martin, with just "London, London, London". I simply dropped the radio handset, shoved my head out of the bunker, which fortunately overlooked the gun line, and bellowed "London". That scene, snapshot if you like, is still clearly etched in my memory. The gunners were all sitting around in the sun, talking, shaving and relaxing. The sergeant in charge of one of the two guns was drinking a mug of tea. Somewhere in the regulations there was a rule, I believe, that, in the absence of a gunner officer, only a major or above could actually give the order for guns to fire. The sergeant was a practical soldier; he knew me and the battalion, and if the adjutant of the Baluchis called for a DF SOS task, he did not quibble. In one swift movement he dropped his tea, flung himself forward on to the lanyard, which, when pulled, fired the twenty-five pounder and away went the first round. Although I was not watching him, the sergeant of the other gun was nearly as quick. The gun crews reacted equally splendidly and there was hardly a pause between the remaining two rounds per guns thundering away. I called up A Company again; Clifford Martin had left his Company HQ, but I stayed glued to the set in case he called again.

The Japanese had mounted a determined dawn attack in some strength and, at the time of Clifford's call, were coming through the small amount of wire which had been carried all that way and set up in front of the position – and a Japanese officer's sword was sharp enough to cut through it. "London" hit them absolutely right in the open, causing heavy casualties and broke up the attack. A minute or so later they would have been through and our company in dire straits, if not overwhelmed. Thanks to "London" and some very soldierly stuff by Clifford Martin and A Company, the attack was repelled with considerable Japanese casualties and they withdrew. Clifford deservedly won the first of his two Military Crosses.

This was a small routine incident of the war in Burma, but it has always stuck in my mind as a superb example of gunner/infantry cooperation. It also puts a very special connotation on the word "London" for me, and even more so for Clifford Martin.

Chapter 7

Commanding Officer

No account of my war service in the Indian Army would be complete without a tribute to Lieutenant Colonel Lindsay, christened Pooler Leman, but widely and affectionately known as Pat, under whom I served, first as a rifle company commander in the latter stages of the Retreat from Burma in 1942 and then, on arrival back in India, as Adjutant for two years, until he left the Battalion on promotion to Brigadier in May 1944.

Pat Lindsay was a member of a well-known Ulster family who had over the years provided imperial administrators – soldiers, judges and the like. Born in 1899, he was commissioned into the 130th Baluchis (later 5th Battalion Baluch Regiment) in 1918, the youngest infantry subaltern in the Indian Army and in time to see some fighting in the closing stages of Allenby's campaign in Palestine and Syria. Between the wars he served almost exclusively on regimental duty, much of it on active service on the North-West Frontier. Although not, as he would have been the first to admit, an intellectual soldier or even Staff College material, he had, by the time he was flown into Burma in March 1942 to take over command of our shattered Battalion, two priceless qualities – a profound knowledge of regimental soldiering and an even more profound knowledge of the Indian soldier and how to lead and handle him.

He proved to be a sound, firm commander on the long wearisome slog out of Burma which involved us in little fighting but considerable hardship and prolonged thirst-ridden marching and digging, often under air attack. On arrival in Imphal, instead of

37

being withdrawn to India immediately, as were many of the battalions, we were sent, all 150 of us, to join the North Assam Brigade on the Ledo road, housed in a pestilential bamboo-hutted camp, where the monsoon and the mosquito, in the absence of anti-malaria drugs and even mosquito nets, caused havoc to the health of men already weakened by months of privation and inadequate rations. When we finally reached Ranchi in Eastern India in September 1942 we were in pretty poor shape, physically and mentally. For example, the Pathan Company, whose company commander and all but one of its VCOs were dead or missing (and that one had to be kicked out for cowardice) had had to be disarmed and were almost in a state of moral collapse. To add to Pat Lindsay's problems, we were given a new and experimental role as a Reconnaissance Battalion organized on four companies: two on an all-jeep basis and two mounted on ponies. This required a substantial number of men (and some officers) to be given extensive equitation training, as well as the working out of battle drills and tactics (such as how many ponies could one horse-holder handle when a section was in action dismounted? How do you organize Battalion Headquarters and the heavy support weapons such as mortars and medium machine guns so that they can operate sometimes on a jeep basis and sometimes on a mounted infantry basis?) Pat Lindsay set about this formidable task with great vigour and imagination.

In any organization, most of all in the close-knit brotherhood of an infantry battalion, when things go wrong everyone closes ranks. There is a strong desire to handle matters within the battalion family and not to wash dirty linen in view of the outside world. Sometimes this is right; more often than not sweeping dirt under the carpet eventually leads to a worse final situation than if the dirt had been thoroughly and publicly cleaned out in the first place. This was the dilemma facing Pat Lindsay. During the Retreat a few men had deserted; there had been the disgraceful incident when a dozen or so Pathans held in a reinforcement camp, prior to being sent to rejoin the Battalion, had been actively encouraged to desert by a Pathan havildar. Most of us were disposed simply to discharge those men, but Pat Lindsay would have none of it. He was determined to and he did, court-martial every single one, including the Havildar. He was resolute in believing, and he was absolutely right,

1. The Author in 1943.

2. Subedar Lal Khan.

3. 7th Battalion, 10th Baluch Regiment Officers and Viceroy's Commissioned Officers Ahmadnagar, October 1941. *(Front row:)* A/Capt. S.M.V. Krishnan (RMO), 2/Lt. G.L. Holden, A/Capt. A.P. Turner, A/Capt. C.H. Mercer, Major C.J. Dyer, Lt. Col. C.J.D. Tomkins, Subedar Major Kirpa Ram Bahadur OBI, T/Capt. P.O. Dunn, 2/Lt. J.P. Randle, 2/Lt. R. MacLean (visiting from Bde HQ), 2/Lt. Irshad Ahmad Khan. *(Second row:) Left:* A/Capt. R.H. Gillett, 2/Lt. J.P.C. Jervis. *Right:* 2/Lt. W.B. Cayley, A/Capt. H.B. Toothill. *Back row: 3rd from left:* Jemadar/Subedar Sohan Lal. *2nd from right:* Subedar Moghal Baz. *Second row: 3rd from left:* Subedar Mehr Khan, *6th from left:* Subedar Ghulam Yasim, *8th from left:* Jemadar Bazar Khan. *Not present:* 2/Lt. C.R.L. Coubrough (on Sigs course at Poona); Capt. Siri Kanth Korla (on duty in Middle East), 2/Lt. O. Greenwood (not yet joined).

4. Charles Coubrough, Ahmadnagar, October 1941.

5. Naik Amir Khan who won a posthumous IOM at Pa-an on 12 February 1942.

6. The Retreat form Burma, 1942. Kalewa. *Standing:* George Holden, Author, Burmese Interpreter, Bill Greenwood. *Seated:* Pat Lindsay.

7. The Retreat from Burma, 1942. On the Indo/Burmese border. Sepoy Allah Dad, the Author, Dan Pettigrew, Siri.

8. Pat Lindsay, 1942.

9. Jock Price, Denys Andrews, "Fish" Herring, Clifford Martin, Shillong, October 1943.

10. Tommy Bruin.

11. Just after the capture of Pegu, May 1945. Clockwise from "Dodgy" Som Dutt (receiving mug), "Eno" Singha, Author, Joe Hudson, "Dizzy" King, FOO, Roderick Maclean, Siri, Clifford Martin, Jock Price.

12. "The Baron" and
    Norrie Waddell,
    Kyaikto,
    September 1945.

13. The Author, Jimmy Whelan, Jock Price, Tony Davies, Kyaikto, February 1946.

14. Old Comrades meet at Baluch Regimental Centre, Abbottabad, January 1976. Clifford Martin, the Author, Subedar Lal Khan.

15. In Moghal Baz's village, Chamderi, North-West Frontier, January 1976. The Author and Subedar Moghal Baz.

16. Delhi, January 1976. Siri, Pat Dunn, Clifford Martin.

17. After the last parade of the Burma Star Association, London, May 2001.
Left to right: Allan Rowley (5/10 Baluch), the Author, Mike Farrant (14/10 Baluch),
Clifford Martin, Charles Coubrough, Ronnie Corson (14/10 Baluch), Tommy Bruin.

that every man in the Battalion should know that desertion was the deadliest of all soldierly sins and would be heavily punished.

It must be remembered that to the Indian soldier his "izzat", his personal honour, was the mainspring of his moral motivation. A man convicted of desertion would be for ever disgraced in his village and his community. It had to be driven home that battle discipline, even wounds or death, were preferable to loss of "izzat". And so a dozen men were court-martialled and sentenced to varying degrees of penal servitude. The Havildar was sentenced to death, but this was commuted by General Headquarters Delhi to penal servitude for life. Before the war this would have meant the penal settlement in the Andaman Islands, but as those had been occupied by the Japs, it meant Multan, reputed to be the hottest and most godforsaken place in India. To drive it home Pat Lindsay staged a dramatic promulgation of sentence. The whole Battalion, now built up by reinforcements to a strength of about 700, was paraded on three sides of a square. Into the middle, in chains, was brought the disgraced Havildar. I, as Adjutant, was ordered to read out the sentence in Urdu, but Pat Lindsay ordered me to pause after the death sentence was read out – and there was a vast gasp of "Wa" from the assembled battalion – before going on to read out the commutation. How right he was was proved by the fact that we had no more desertion in nearly three more years of fighting in Burma.

When I took over as Adjutant I was still only 20, with only nine months service and with virtually no knowledge of military paper work and administration, and therefore very very green. Pat Lindsay, though a hard task-master, was good to me, helped and encouraged me, and so with the added help and advice of a new staff-trained 2IC, I slogged away to get a reasonably good show going.

In two ways I did not find Pat Lindsay an easy man to serve. Firstly, he was not at his friendliest before breakfast and, as we hacked round together on our ponies, I had to bear the brunt of this. However, I soon realized, as he grew more cordial as the day went on and was friendliness itself in the Mess of an evening meal that this was just him; it then ceased to worry me. Secondly, he was a very hard task-master in every aspect of the Battalion's life and training, discipline, turnout, mess and quarter guard standards. He

39

really gripped the Battalion and that meant that I, as Adjutant, had loyally to pass on a lot of fairly tough, often unwelcome, orders. The more perceptive officers realized the good sense of this; others did not and among some I was not the most popular officer in the Battalion. I began to learn a little tact and diplomacy, but I did find that giving him my unswerving loyalty demanded much determination on my part.

As I came to know him better, I got to admire him more, because I realized that he was essentially a kind, thoughtful and understanding man, without personal ambition for his own advancement, and would always fight for his battalion, even if it involved the displeasure of his superiors. He confided in me quite a lot and once said to me, "You know, John, they can sack me tomorrow. I'm not a rich man but I can always get by". In fact with his Irish charm, his great conviviality off duty and the wonders he did with the Battalion, he became one of the characters of the Division. One day a stray staff Brigadier arrived unheralded and demanded to see something. Pat was polite but firm. "Whilst it is very nice to see you, Brigadier, I do not recall you making an appointment, to visit my Battalion. I am very sorry to say that it is not convenient." He got away with it and, as a result of his bluff ways, Brigade and Divisional Headquarters did not mess us about unduly, because they knew that he would not stand for it. In a lighthearted way his great adversary was the senior medical officer of the Division, a genial southern Irishman who was always complaining about our hygiene. With six hundred ponies or mules tethered out in the open in a tropical climate, it was not really surprising. His great joke was that if he didn't know where the Baluchis were on the Divisional front, he just scanned the horizon with his binoculars and wherever he saw a particularly large cloud of flies, that was where we would be! Out of the line and off duty, he and Pat Lindsay would frequently meet at the club, with much Hibernian repartee of the "Pat, you're from the Black North" variety, swiftly parried by "It's your misfortune, Bill, to come from the Dirty South!" Off parade Pat Lindsay was gregarious and convivial and had a professional fighting man's capacity for lowering the hard stuff. Even by Indian Army officers' drinking standards, ours, once out of the line, was formidable. While I enjoyed a party, I found that I simply could not keep up with this and cope with my busy job as Adjutant, so I tended to opt out. Pat Lindsay was of the old school and, despite lowering substantial amounts, was never the worse for drink. The convention of those days was that drink taken could never be an excuse for lack of good manners nor for failing to be on parade and being capable of doing one's job bang on time the next morning. Pat ensured that this convention was strictly observed.

We had some amusing experiences. In Ranchi, not long after we had started our mounted infantry training, we were warned that Wavell, then Commander-in-Chief, India, was coming to visit us at a certain hour. On the day Wavell committed the unforgivable sin of arriving fifteen minutes early (I discovered afterwards that he often did it on purpose, just to see how quick on their toes a unit was). I got the message from the Quarter Guard and rushed to tell Pat. "My God, John! Get down as quickly as you can to D Company and tell Pat (the Company Commander) to get them on parade!" I did just that and, as the great man arrived, D Company, more like a horde of Tartar horsemen than a mounted infantry company, swept by. Wavell surveyed them quizzically with his one good eye. "Not much skill, but plenty of spirit!" was his laconic comment. I exchanged glances with Pat, all was well.

On New Year's Eve 1942 we all went for a monumental party at the Ranchi Club. Well into the early hours of 1 January 1943 Pat Lindsay, on his way out of the club, paused to try the fruit machine with a few spare annas. By sheer luck he hit the jackpot and the machine poured out a vast flood of coins. Pat, in sparkling form, scooped up these coins in his large fist bellowing "Bearer, Bearer" at the top of his voice. He then flung them around the club, handful by handful, whereupon not only every bearer in the club, but every bhisti, masalchi, dhobi, sweeper, mali, chowkidar in and around the club leapt off their charpoys and joined in a mad scramble, wildly encouraged by every Baluchi officer present. The chaos was colossal. Pat Lindsay and the rest of us departed, chuckling, into the night.

After four months in Ranchi we moved back up the line to Imphal, but after three months there it was realized that, despite our work and enthusiasm, we needed a further period of training outside an operational area. We were then sent for six months to

Shillong, an agreeable hill station in Assam in North-East India, albeit very wet indeed in the South-West Monsoon.

Two personal anecdotes from those times illustrate Pat's wisdom and understanding. I had applied for a Regular Commission and was called for an interview with a Selection Board, chaired by a Major General. Pat Lindsay had to write a report on me, but all he wrote was "This officer is my Adjutant". I was somewhat concerned at its brevity, but in fact I need not have worried. Pat Lindsay knew his military world and when I was called before the General, his opening words were "Well, if you are Pat Lindsay's Adjutant, you must be good enough for a Regular Commission and how is your Colonel?" The rest of the interview was spent talking about Pat and I got my Regular Commission.

Shillong had all the usual facilities of an Indian Hill Station, a club, golf course, hotels, a cinema. It also had the Welsh Mission, which worked wonders among the local pagan hill tribe, the Khasis, teaching them English, western standards of hygiene and training the beautiful fair-skinned Khasi girls, (some of the most nubile girls most of us had ever seen), to be nurses in the first-class hospital there. So beautiful were these girls that some became the mistresses of young bachelor planters in the tea-gardens of Assam. Two such comely girls returned to Shillong when their patrons went to war, were generously paid off and were living each in her own comfortable bungalow. Bill Greenwood, also now a captain, who had been my company officer in the early fighting in Burma, and I reckoned that our chances of surviving the next and fairly imminent encounter with the Japs were not too good and, preferring the pleasures of the flesh to the alternative pleasures of the bottle or Bridge, took on one each of these two girls as our mistresses. Most days after dinner in the Mess basha Bill and I set out on our motor bikes for a rewarding evening with our girls. I am pretty certain that Pat Lindsay knew what we were up to, but he probably shared our assessment of our survival chances and, being a man of the world, was not disposed to interfere, providing we were discreet (which we were) and it did not interfere with our work (which it did not). A less understanding and human man would have waxed sententious and pompous.

Twice whilst serving him as Adjutant I was, for almost the only two occasions in my life, seriously ill, once with pleurisy as a result of the Retreat and in late 1943, just as we were going back into Burma, with a really bad go of jaundice. On both occasions I was away, with sick leave, for over a month and on both occasions he kept my job open for me and thus saved me from the Depot or some training job away from proper active service.

At the end of 1943, now better able to cope with our Reconnaissance Battalion role, we left Shillong and rejoined the Division in the Chin Hills at heights about 8,000 feet and about 170 miles south of Imphal. As an operational Battalion Commander, Pat Lindsay was a sound, unflappable tactician. At that time and in the Division's subsequent fighting withdrawal to Imphal, it was very much a company commanders' battle, and he was served by very fine rifle company commanders.

When General Slim realized the full extent of the Japanese threat to Imphal and Kohima, and indeed to India, the Division was hurriedly withdrawn into the Imphal Box. This involved alternate spells of very hard fighting and some equally testing forced marches. A divisional lay-back position was formed at a place called Tonzang, hence Tonforce, with Baluchis, West Yorks and Gurkhas all under Pat's command and, despite substantial losses, acquitted itself well in some tough fighting. Pat Lindsay was by then aged 45, quite old for the sheer physical demands of those sort of operations. As Adjutant I realized that, if he attempted to march, he would simply not be able to cope and, after a great deal of resistance from him, I persuaded him to travel by jeep, whilst Jock Price the Intelligence Officer and I marched with Battalion Headquarters. Finally, nearing Imphal, I heard that the Divisional Commander was standing a mile ahead to watch our brigade enter the Divisional Box. I suggested to Pat that he got out of his jeep and lead us back, much to the delight of the whole Battalion. I heard afterwards that the Divisional Commander was full of praise of "Good old Pat Lindsay, marched all that way!" We loved Pat for it.

Shortly afterwards, with Pat's two years in command at an end, a new Commanding Officer, Lieutenant Colonel Maurice Wright, arrived and Pat went off on well-deserved promotion to command a newly raised Brigade in India. We were truly sad to see him go.

On Indian Independence in 1947 Pat retired and for the next forty years lived in a village in Suffolk, with his wife, Mary, supported by his two sons, Patrick and Richard. There he devoted himself to service to the community: Church Warden, County Councillor and later Chairman of the Council, Governor of a school, etc. He also played a leading part in the affairs of his old Regiment's Dinner Club in England, especially in helping the widows of officers of the Regiment. For many years we officers of his old battalion had an annual reunion which he never missed. On and off I saw a good deal of him and he always introduced me, "This is John Randle, my old Adjutant".

His character much impressed me. I admired him for the way that he rebuilt the Battalion, eschewing easy popularity and, having weighed up the situation, strove for the good of the battalion at the risk of his own advancement, scorning currying favour with higher authority, and yet at the same time he was essentially a kind, warm-hearted man. The Battalion finished the war in 1945 as arguably one of the best battalions in the crack 17th Indian Division, and the cornerstone of our success was due to the foundation that he had laid.

In October 1988 he died in his 90th year. There was a moving service in his village church, with a full congregation, including Clifford Martin and myself. His two sons paid me the great compliment of inviting me to give an address about his life as a soldier. I look back to him down the years with profound respect and affection.

D. Background Events

March–August 1944

In March 1944 the Battalion, with the rest of 17 Division carried out a fighting withdrawal from the Chin Hills into the main 4th Corps defensive box around the key area of Imphal. Because the Corps was completely surrounded by the Japanese and entirely dependent on air supply, our horses and mules were taken away (and presumably used as a meat ration, since they could not be fed) and the Battalion reverted to normal infantry. We therefore, despite all the hard work and enthusiasm, were never able to operate as a Reconnaissance Battalion. In retrospect I think that the concept was flawed. In jungle and forest reconnaissance had to be done on foot. Once out on the open plains of Burma in 1945 armoured cars, with their greater fire power and better communications, proved to be very effective.

In May the Battalion was in Divisional reserve (see Chapter 8), but during June was involved in the cauldron of the fighting on the Silchar track above Bishenpur. As Battle Adjutant, nowadays Operations Officer, I, with the Intelligence Officer, Jock Price, controlled the Battalion radio command net and the immensely complicated fire support arrangements in conjunction with the Gunners – our own support weapons, medium, field and mountain guns, heavy mortars and MMGs. In late June we shared a Command Post with 2/5th Gurkhas and I built up a good rapport with their Battle Adjutant, Pat Gouldsbury (See Appx A). The Battalion paper war was run by the 2IC back at B Echelon (the area in the rear where non-essential vehicles, stores and the administrative elements were located, usually under Brigade control) in Imphal.

Chapter 8

RED HILL

Between March and July 1944 the epic Battle of Imphal, the key battle of the whole Burma Campaign, was fought out in all its bloody ferocity. Although the loss of Kohima would have been serious, the loss of Imphal, with its airfield, stores and depots, the keystone in preventing any serious Japanese incursion of north-east India and the springboard for an advance back into Burma, would have been catastrophic. The Japanese knew this and made Imphal their principal objective. To that end they deployed their crack 33rd Division on the main axis up the Tiddim-Imphal road from the south. The 33rd Division had been the main opponent of our 17th Indian Division in the thrashing that we had had in the 1942 Retreat. Their 214th Regiment had the nickname of "The White Tigers", but in later years this has tended to become associated with the whole 33rd Division. Back in 1942 a competition had been held to decide on an appropriate divisional sign for 17th Indian Division. The flippantly popular suggestion was a "Blue-Arsed Fly on a Green Background" to denote the extent to which we were buzzing about all over South-East Asia. In the end the modest suggestion of the Divisional Commander's wife for a black cat found favour.

33rd Division, having harassed 17th Indian Division all the way back from Tiddim, finally, during March and early April, closed up on our main defensive positions in and around Bishenpur, some seventeen miles south of Imphal. 17th Division, being at that time a Light Division of only two brigades, was reinforced by a brigade from the 20th Indian Division. By late April the ring was thus set

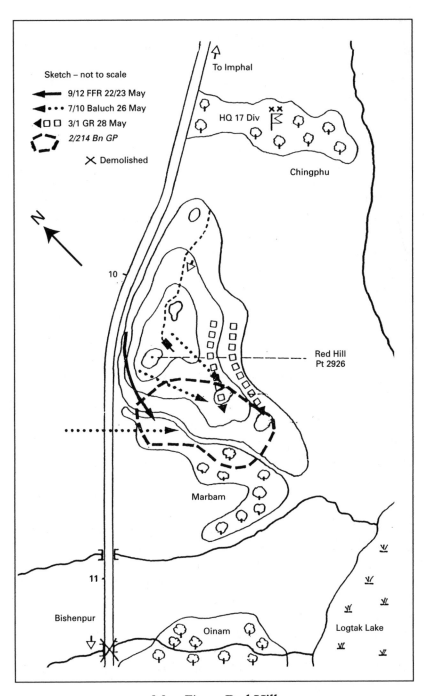

for a classic fight to the finish between the White Tigers and the Black Cats. The Battle of Red Hill was just a small part of the bloody tapestry of that fight. It was nevertheless an interesting encounter on two counts – a most unusual tactical setting and a classic example of the courage and formidable fighting skill of Japanese infantrymen and gunners.

Initially the Division, with its attached Brigade, was exposed to the usual Japanese tactic of a holding frontal attack, linked to flanking attacks. Since the Logtak Lake to the east of the road was impassable, the Japanese made thrusts along the line of hills to the west. Divisional Headquarters was located near the village of Chingphu and just to the north-east of a hill feature, on the east side of the Tiddim-Imphal road at Milestone 10, which became known as Red Hill because of the reddish-brown nature of its soil. 7th/10th Baluchis, hitherto the Divisional Reconnaissance Battalion, having just had its horses and mules removed, was the Divisional Reserve, based in Imphal. However, Battalion HQ and one Company (D Company: Joe Hudson) were sent forward between Chingphu and Red Hill to bolster up the local defence of Divisional Headquarters. Someone (I think it was Maurice Wright, our newly appointed Commanding Officer) had the prescience and soldierly foresight to deploy one platoon of D Company, under Subedar Ghulam Yasin, on Point 2926 the highest part of Red Hill. Fortunately the latter was an experienced and unflappable soldier.

On the night of 20/21 May, with the monsoon intensifying, the Japanese made their most ambitious and daring thrust. 2nd Battalion, 214th Regiment Group, moved several miles along the hills, crossed the road and endeavoured to seize the whole Red Hill feature. The group consisted of about 500 infantry, 100 gunners with three light-calibre guns and 40 sappers, who on the way demolished the bridge and laid mines on the road to the west of Oinam. Only Ghulam Yasin's platoon was there to thwart them and he fought an all-night battle with great courage and professional skill. Early on he sensed that he was in for a long fight and applied rigid fire control to conserve his ammunition. Despite repeated attacks, the platoon held out and at dawn the Japanese had to dig in on the southern part of the feature and in part of the small village of Marbam to the south. Down below on the north-east side of the hill we in Battalion Headquarters and the rest of D

Company stood to during the night, but Maurice Wright wisely decided that it would be imprudent to try and reinforce Ghulam Yasin's platoon in the middle of such night fighting. The Baluchis' successful denial of Point 2926 to the Japs turned out to be the critical factor in the outcome of the battle.

Next morning, from their position, the Japanese could bring fire to bear on the road and so 17th Division Headquarters was in the unenviable position of having a Japanese Battalion between it and its forward Brigades, artillery and administrative units, itself under threat of attack, and its main artery forward cut.

On 21 May Divisional Headquarters, initially underestimating the enemy strength on Red Hill and thinking it was only a fighting patrol, ordered the Divisional Defence Platoon to counter-attack and drive the Japanese off. It was a classic case of using a nut to crack a sledge-hammer and was a costly failure. Also on the 21st, four tanks sent back from Bishenpur were knocked out or held up at Oinam, but the enemy were engaged by the Divisional Artillery, which had to "about-face" in its positions at Bishenpur. On 22 May a battalion group of 9th/12th Frontier Force Regiment from Corps Reserve put in several costly and unsuccessful attempts from the north-west. On the 24th a convoy ran the gauntlet of Japanese fire to get rations and sorely needed ammunition to Bishenpur and the remainder of my Battalion was ordered up from Imphal. On 25 May Maurice Wright was ordered to put in a full battalion attack to recapture the Red Hill feature.

This was not only his first battle in command, but his first battle ever. He planned it with professional skill. The lie of the land and the enemy dispositions only appeared to allow two feasible lines of attack other than the axis of the failed Frontier Force attack. Plan A was to have carried out a long night approach march from north-east of Red Hill, then well to the west of the road south-westward parallel to the road, a swing to the east, and forming up in the sodden paddy to the south-west of Red Hill, with an assault north-eastwards through the enemy-occupied Marbam village and up the slopes. This, probably in heavy monsoon rain, would have tested a battalion that had practised, and even rehearsed, such an attack. As night attacks had not been foreseen as a role for a Reconnaissance Battalion and we had not trained for it, Maurice wisely discarded it for something simpler, albeit with some snags.

Plan B was an approach march up the north-east side of Red Hill, a start line astride the summit based on the secure D Company Platoon, and an assault southward down the hill on to the enemy dug in there. The ground did not allow for more than two companies, A Company (Clifford Martin) and C Company (Denys Andrews) to be so deployed, and so B Company (Roderick Maclean) was to put in an attack from the road eastward on to Marbam village. Maurice wisely opted for Plan B, the attack to go in just after first light on 26 May.

In the early hours of the 26th in torrential rain Tactical Battalion Headquarters, consisting of Maurice Wright, Jock Price, a signaller with a radio and me, climbed up to set up shop with the D Company platoon on the top of Red Hill. Jock and I manned the Battalion command net from a slit trench half-full of water with a groundsheet over the radio to try and keep it dry and functioning. The pungent aroma of a dead Jap a few feet away added to the charm of the occasion. Once the battle got going at dawn quite a lot of flak was whizzing over the top of the hill, so we didn't stand around. Fortunately from the top radio communications were quite good and we were able to keep Maurice and his escort, in another slit trench nearby, informed of the progress of B Company. The progress of A and C Companies just below could be seen from the top. It had been prudently decided that fire support from the Divisional artillery at Bishenpur ran too great a risk of causing casualties to our deployment, and was ruled out. The Battalion mortars, under Jimmy Whelan, were however used from base plate positions south-west of Chingphu.

The attack went in as planned and was pressed with great courage. Some ground both on the hill and in Marbam was taken but the enemy was not dislodged. Apart from the Pa-an fighting in February 1942, this was our costliest battle with 140 casualties, including two officers and a Jemadar killed, and two officers, Clifford Martin and his company officer, Tommy Bruin, wounded. Ghulam Yasin worthily won an MC for his gallant defence of Pt 2926, Clifford Martin a Bar to his MC and Naik Sarfraz Khan, a posthumous IDSM (Indian Distinguished Service Medal) for successfully wiping out a bunker. Sadly Ghulam Yasin was killed three weeks later when our Medium gunners dropped a 5.5 inch shell short on his position. Something during the battle went wrong with the leadership of one of C Company's platoon and Denys Andrews was not an entirely happy man. Sadly he too was killed in action on 6 June, so I never knew the full story.

On 28 May 3rd/1st Gurkhas from 20th Division put in an attack, on a new untried axis, again unsuccessfully and with heavy losses, including the Commanding Officer, Adjutant and two Company Commanders killed, but during that night the Japanese finally pulled out.

It was not fashionable in those days to heap praise on our enemy and it has not really been fashionable since. Nevertheless, to my mind the exploit of that Japanese battalion in holding out for so long against repeated attacks was one of the finest feats of arms that I ever saw. There was much to dislike and despise about the way the Japs conducted the war, but no one who actually fought them on the battlefield could deny their courage and fighting prowess. For a week they had dug in and held that position under constant artillery and mortar fire, with no reinforcements nor resupply of food or ammunition, and no succour for their wounded; they repelled three attacks, well mounted by seasoned battalions and bravely pressed, and inflicted heavy casualties on us. Of the 640 men of the group who had set out on 20 May only thirty-seven returned who were capable of fighting.

The last word must surely be with General Slim, the commander of 14th Army, who, after visiting the recaptured Red Hill, praised their courage. No soldier who fought in Burma on either side could ask for higher praise than that.

The fighting around Bishenpur and the Silchar track went on, in its bloody intensity, for another six weeks and it is some measure of that intensity that four VCs were won there. The Black Cats finally triumphed over the White Tigers who were not only fought to a standstill but destroyed as a fighting formation.

In the 1990s the All Burma Veteran Association of Japan (ABVAJ), the equivalent of our Burma Star Association, with the support of the Japanese Government, obtained the permission of the Indian Government to erect a memorial at Imphal, in memory of all the 190,000 Japanese dead in the whole Burma Campaign. The site chosen for this memorial was Red Hill, the nearest point to Imphal that the Japanese ever reached. A Service of Reconciliation took place there in 2001 attended by the ABVAJ and the (British) Burma Campaign Fellowship Group (BCFG) (see Appendix C). Old Black Cats and old White Tigers were among those present. I was privileged to receive an invitation to be included in the BCFG party, with all expenses paid, but for domestic reasons was unable to accept.

Chapter 9

A Very Brave Decision

It is a platitude that, of the two sorts of courage, physical and moral, the latter is the much more important and that men can often have physical courage and yet lack moral courage, but seldom does a man with moral courage lack physical courage. This is a tale of moral courage in battle.

In the summer of 1944, during the monsoon, my battalion was involved in the great Battle of Imphal when the Japanese made their final thrust to drive the British back from the Assam/Burma border with the ultimate aim of advancing into India. Our tough old Commanding Officer, Pat Lindsay, to whom I had been Company Commander/Adjutant for two years and with whom I had developed a considerable rapport, was promoted to command a brigade in India and a new commanding officer, straight from an office desk in GHQ Delhi, arrived. Maurice Wright was a very different sort of man and I found it difficult to serve him as loyally and as happily as I had done his predecessor. In fact he was, some weeks later, to sack me, not because I had failed him or the Battalion in any way, but simply due to our incompatibility, though he was generous enough to "kick me upstairs" and give me command of a rifle company, which suited me fine. In general I and others in the Battalion found him a little lacking in human under-standing and a sense of humour, and, above all, perhaps not unnaturally, he found the appalling conditions of trench warfare against some very tough Japanese, under monsoon conditions, in contrast to the comfort of an office and bungalow in Delhi, extremely difficult to adapt to. Nevertheless I blame myself for this failure, as it was up to me, despite my youth and lack of experience, to adapt myself to my new Commanding Officer's ways and not the other way round.

One of the problems for a Commanding Officer in battle was the Standard Operating Procedure (SOP) then in force, that the Second-in-Command was Left out of Battle (LOB), and so was often not seen for days, but kept the paper war going in the rear areas. This, however, meant that the Commanding Officer had no confidant with whom to discuss things and a 22-year-old acting Captain could not really fill the bill, especially for a somewhat introverted man. Later, as a Company Commander to him, both in the closing stages of the Battle of Imphal, on training and finally in the heavy fighting for Meiktila in March 1945, I found him utterly different and we got on well. He had a clear tactical brain, gave good, lucid, short orders, never flapped and had an uncanny knack of always being available if one wanted help or advice. He never interfered or breathed down one's neck and gave the impression that one had his complete confidence. Above all, he believed in getting up right forward to see things for himself. He was one of those men whose whole personality changed under the stimulus of battle. The contrast between serving him as Adjutant and as a Company Commander was considerable. Although I never felt for him the warmth that I had had for his predecessor, I had profound respect for his leadership qualities in battle. The following is a short illustration of his great quality of moral courage.

The 1944 Japanese offensive reached its crescendo and our forces were continually having to plug gaps as the enemy outflanked our positions in their desperate efforts to reach the key areas of the town of Imphal with its airfield and its supply installations. The battalion, with myself then Battle Adjutant, was sent off on one of those "ad hoc" forces which were so fashionable in the Second World War, called "Lakri-force" simply because "Lakri" (Urdu for Wood) was the nickname of a Brigadier Wood. The Japanese had seized a key feature, a narrow saddle-backed hill, and we were warned that we would probably have to assault it, drive them off and then hold the feature ourselves. Maurice Wright, as usual, decided to go and see the ground for himself and came back to the Battalion Headquarters dug-out looking somewhat glum. Because we were in static positions and because radio communications

54

under monsoon conditions were far from reliable, telephone line communication with Lakri-force Headquarters was used. He ordered me to get through to the Brigade Major so that he could then ask the Brigade Major to put him through to the Brigade Commander. Maurice Wright had a telephone in his next-door dug out, on the same line as the telephone in the Operations dug-out from where I operated. I duly got him through to the Brigade Major, who in turn put him through to the Brigadier. I decided, rightly or wrongly, to listen into the conversation, not so much out of idle curiosity but because the sooner I knew what was afoot the earlier I would be able to arrange an orders group of the necessary company commanders, gunners etc, arrange maps, meals, ammunition and so on. Maurice came straight to the point. "Sir, I have been up to that position and it is my firm belief that to attack it frontally would be utterly suicidal, stand very little chance of success and involve a very high casualty rate. The ground and our dispositions do not, as you know, allow any flanking attack." The Brigade Commander, not unnaturally, was highly displeased with this. "Are you telling me that your battalion is not prepared to attack this position?" "Yes, sir, I am." "In that case I shall have to ask the Frontier Force to do it."

This may not appear to be out of the ordinary, but in fact it was a display of exceptional moral courage by Maurice Wright. He was newly arrived and therefore an unknown quality. In this sort of fighting, brigade, battalion and company commanders were dispensable and were frequently sacked on the spot for failure in, or lack of zeal for, battle. Had he been a long-standing commanding officer who had established a reputation for himself, this might have been different, but he was not, and I expected the Brigadier to arrive quite shortly and sack him on the spot. Evidently Maurice Wright was only too aware of this, as though, unlike Pat Lindsay, he did not discuss it with me or say anything about it, (possibly because he was unaware that I had heard what had gone on), he was on a particularly short fuse. However, nothing happened. Next day another battalion of the Brigade, whose commanding officer had clearly not gone up forward as Maurice had done, put in an attack and, as the latter had forecast, was unsuccessful, with very heavy casualties. I believe, though I am not certain, that the Brigadier did at least have the honesty to tell Maurice that he had wished that he had accepted his advice.

Despite my personal difficulties with Maurice Wright, my opinion of him went up enormously. I felt it only right discreetly to let the Company Commander, who would have been involved in the attack, know the strength of character and moral courage that Maurice had shown. It speaks much for the good sense of the British/Indian Army that the following year, as a result of the Battalion's success in battle, he was promoted to command another brigade in the Division. His actions that day at Imphal, when he was so new in command, have remained with me always as a fine example of unselfishness and moral courage.

Chapter 10

A Latter-Day Gunga Din

Most people of my own and earlier generations are familiar with Kipling's ballad about the heroic water carrier Gunga Din and its famous last line "You're a better man than I am, Gunga Din!" This is a true tale of an even more remarkable Indian follower.

It is necessary to explain the background of that most prosaic and indelicate of subjects, the sanitary arrangements in India and of the Indian Army. Apart from the houses of the wealthier, hotels and clubs in the big cities, there was no waterborne sanitation in India and everyone was dependent upon the good old-fashioned privy or, among the more well-to-do, an old-fashioned commode, serviced by a sanitary man known universally as a sweeper. In the Indian Army, with somewhat heavy irony, the sweepers were often called "mehtar"- prince. Among the predominantly Hindu population of India with its rigid caste system, all people engaged in menial tasks of this nature came from a class known as "The Untouchables" and, to a strict Hindu, contact with, or even the shadow of, an Untouchable was ritual defilement. Among Moslems and other faiths, although they did not have the same rigid caste system, sweepers were regarded as the lowest of the low.

There were two personal taboos which were clearly put over to all British officers on joining the Indian Army – firstly, that one should on no account ever show oneself naked to one's men (the British Army practice of the officers and men all stripping off and plunging into the sea or into a river was "out"). The second was that excretion should be done in complete privacy and certainly not in the presence of one's soldiers. This practice was maintained even

57

on active service, unless in close contact with the enemy, and one used the officers' mess commode or thunder box which was usually dug down and covered over, and was serviced by the officers' mess sweeper in Battalion Headquarters. Under battle conditions, away with one's company, one obviously did as everybody else did and went out discreetly, clear of the front line, with a shovel. In a prolonged static battle this was often inadvisable and arrangements had to be made within the defensive system.

During much of the fighting in Burma our officers' mess sweeper was a diminutive man called Kantu. He was an enlisted follower; not armed, but accompanied the Battalion wherever it went and was subject to military law. He was a delightful little man, always smiling, always smart, and took particular pride in his job; so much so that it was somewhat disconcerting, when one had barely finished one's daily offering to hear and see it being whipped away in preparation for the next arrival. During the after-breakfast period he was always on duty near the officers' mess thunder box tent or dug-out and on several occasions when one approached it he would come smartly to attention, tuck his sweeper's brush under his left armpit, as an officer might his cane, in the days when officers carried a cane, and give an immaculate salute with the words "Commanding Officer sahib, pot par hai". (The Commanding Officer is on the pot) or "Smith sahib, pot par hai" etc.

In 1944 the battalion was back in Assam and Burma for the second time and involved in the very heavy fighting at Imphal. In the latter stages of that battle we were just above a place called Bishenpur and, because of the severity of the fighting, units had got mixed up. The Japanese were sometimes dug in barely seventy yards from our positions, which were in a series of wired-in picquets, many of which they overlooked, and so could bring direct fire from seventy-five millimetre guns and from small arms on to us; this at times made movement by daylight somewhat hazardous. Battalion Headquarters, at which I was the Battle Adjutant, was with one rifle company and, for some inexplicable reason which I cannot recall, a platoon of the Northamptonshire Regiment, all in one such position. It was the height of the monsoon and for that reason and, because we had been for several months on half-rations of bully beef and biscuits, almost everyone was suffering from diarrhoea in one form or another, including the platoon of the

Northamptons. Sweeper Kantu was there sharing the burden of the day. He had sited the Officers' Mess thunder box in a dug-out, half submerged in water but shielded from any direct Japanese fire. He also dug his own slit trench, which like the rest of them was largely full of water and also a crawl-trench out through the wire into the jungle. After each use of the thunder box he had to crawl away along the trench, often under fire, to deposit the contents in a pit that he had dug. Failure to do this would have immeasurably worsened the appalling sanitary conditions and led to even worse bowel diseases. Normally there were only three or four officers in Battalion Headquarters but with the addition of the platoon of the Northamptons who had asked and received my authority to use our facilities, Kantu was working virtually round the clock in performing his duties. Day after day this humble little man worked away to make this vital contribution, ceaselessly crawling along the exposed trench, with the added risk of being ambushed when he got beyond the wire. He did so without complaint for about a fortnight, until the intensity of the fighting died down.

His conduct so amazed the Northamptons that they asked that his work should be recognized. Here was this humble little man, who had started life probably in as lowly a position as any human being on earth, with no benefit of education, yet he was risking his life day after day to do his little bit of duty as he saw it. It is a very remarkable example of the triumph of the human spirit from a most unlikely source and under appalling conditions. Maurice Wright, having thought deeply about it and having spoken to the Brigadier, decided that he would put Kantu in for a "Mention in Dispatches". This was duly done, with the citation setting out the circumstances. It was without parallel that anyone should get a "Mention" for "shovelling s..t" but this was agreed by 14th Army Commander, that great and understanding soldier Bill Slim, and Kantu was in due course awarded his Mention. It was and remains a heart-warming story.

Kantu survived that campaign and our subsequent advance into Burma and was in due course demobbed. Somehow or other some of us were able to keep track of him and were delighted to hear that he was resettled in his humble home somewhere in what used to be called the United Provinces. Then sadly we heard that, still a comparatively young man, he had died of tuberculosis. I wonder what Kipling would have made of this tale – as fine a story of courage and devotion to duty as I know.

(*This tale originally appeared in* Dekho, *the journal of the Burma Star Association*).

Chapter 11

That Thing (A Clash of Cultures)

In June 1944, at the height of the Battle of Imphal, my battalion of the Baluchis was part of 17th Indian Division, which was slogging it out in the monsoon with the Japanese 33rd Division in the Bishenpur/Silchar Track area south of Imphal. Because 17 Div was then only a Light Division of two Brigades, we had a Brigade of 20th Indian Division under command; that Brigade contained a battalion of the Northamptonshire Regiment. By then, and because of our earlier fighting in the Chin Hills, we had been on half-rations for six months. The fighting was intense and units had become somewhat mixed up in the various wired-in company and platoon redoubts. For some odd reason our Battalion HQ/one rifle company redoubt contained a platoon of the Northamptons under command of a sergeant, and very good they were too, bearing their full share of manning the defences and patrolling.

One afternoon, with the monsoon rain belting down and the fighting quiescent, a runner came to the Battalion Headquarter's command post dug-out with a message from our Subedar Major, Mohammed Khan, to ask if I would please come down to the gap on the south-west side of the perimeter, hidden from enemy view and hence used by all patrols, where my presence was urgently required. It was so exceptional for the Subedar Major to summon the Adjutant, even in very polite terms (he would always come to the Adjutant), that I realized that it must be something out of the ordinary. Leaving Jock Price, the Intelligence Officer, to man the controls, I went down quickly.

When I reached the wire there was indeed a tense situation. Just outside the wire was the platoon sergeant of the Northamptons with a returning patrol from that platoon. Slung on a length of bamboo, carried by a couple of private soldiers, was a wild pig, which somehow or other they had managed to kill or trap whilst out on patrol. Now to them this was a superb bit of good fortune, with one or two delicious meals in prospect; metaphorically their mouths were already watering. However, to the Muslim, be he civilian or soldier, and our Battalion was three-quarters Muslim, a pig was an unclean animal whose presence anywhere near them was a religious defilement.

I spoke first to the Platoon Sergeant whose face was strained with tension and who said, "Sir, you know what the rations are like; we're all hungry, and browned off to hell with bully beef and biscuits. We've had the good luck to catch this pig and I want to bring it inside the perimeter to cook and eat it in our little cook-house area." This was said with a determined and defiant look. I then turned to the Subedar Major, Mohammed Khan, who was with a small group of Punjabi Mussulmans from the rifle company, all standing quietly, but with grim, tense looks. "Sahib, that thing [he could not bring himself to use the word "pig"] is not coming into our position to defile us." Now, it was a very rash and foolish British Officer of the Indian Army who disregarded the advice of the Subedar Major in a religious matter. Everyone, in these conditions, was on a short fuse and a very ugly incident, not excluding bloodshed, was in prospect. I really had not the faintest idea what to do, but felt it was essential to play for time. I told the Platoon Sergeant to order his patrol to stay where they were, but for him alone to come inside the perimeter and talk to me. I ordered the Subedar Major to do the same. Fortunately Mohammed Khan knew no English and the Platoon Sergeant no Urdu. I asked them both quietly to state their views, which they did – with the same vehement stubbornness. Suddenly I saw a glimmer of light. "Supposing," I said to the Platoon Sergeant, "I were to order you to go out on patrol again, well away from the position, butcher the pig there, cut it up into small joints, put them inside the haversacks of the patrol and then return and unpack them, only when you are in the area of your own little cook-house, how would you feel about that?" He thought for a moment and then, to my great relief, said, "I think that would be OK, Sir". I then turned to the Subedar

Major and explained my idea to him. I reminded him that, out of the line and in barracks, British Officers in Indian Regiments ate bacon and other pig products discreetly and that this was tacitly accepted by the Muslim Mess Havildar and other Muslim members of the Mess Staff, sometimes I understood by an additional day of fasting added on to the annual Islamic fast of Ramzan. I assured him that the Platoon Sergeant would honour his side of the bargain strictly to avoid any offence, and that what was hidden in the haversacks of the British patrol was no concern of ours. That wise and experienced old soldier thought quietly for a while and then said that he was satisfied with my proposal, and so it happily turned out – thank God!

The next day the Platoon Sergeant looked in to the Battalion Headquarters dug-out and, seeing I was alone, handed me a small parcel "With the compliments of the Northamptons, Sir". Delivered to our fortunately Christian follower cook, this unexpected gift went down very well for Battalion Headquarters supper that evening, accompanied by some crack about the Adjutant saving his bacon.

(*This tale originally appeared in* Durbar, *the journal of the Indian Military Historical Society*).

E Background Events

August 1944–May 1945

In August 1944 17th Indian Division, having virtually destroyed its old adversary 33rd Division in the fighting at Bishenpur, was relieved by 5th Indian Division and sent to Ranchi in Eastern India for four months' rest and retraining. 7th/10th Baluchis in 63 Indian Brigade were included.

In January 1945 the Division, fully motorized and with an Armoured Brigade, returned to Imphal and then moved in a concealed move down the Kabaw and Myittha Valleys to the Irrawaddy. After 7th Indian Division had secured a bridgehead near Pakokku, 17 Div passed through and made a rapid thrust to Meiktila, which was captured after severe fighting. Road supply was discarded and the Division, reinforced by its third brigade, 99th Indian Brigade, was supplied entirely by air. It was thus able to see off all Japanese counterattacks. 7th/10th Baluchis took a prominent part in the capture of West Meiktila, as a result of which Naik Fazal Din was awarded a posthumous VC and Maurice Wright an immediate DSO, and shortly afterwards was promoted to command 99 Bde in the Division. The 2IC "Dodgy" Som Dutt took over command when the Battalion was involved in the fighting around Pyawbwe and the thrust to Rangoon, including playing a prominent part in the capture of Pegu.

Chapter 12

POINT 900

By early April 1945 17th Indian Division, having successfully captured the key communication centre of Meiktila in Central Burma and, with the aid of its flown-in third brigade, successfully repulsed all Japanese attempts to recapture it, turned its attention to the advance southward to Rangoon. Air reconnaissance and other intelligence indicated that there were strong enemy positions in and around the township of Pyawbwe, some 25 miles south of Meiktila. The main divisional assault was from the north and north-west. 7th/10th Baluchis was, however, given an independent role to make a wide right-flanking advance to seize and hold a prominent hill feature, Point 900, about three miles to the west of Pyawbwe; a squadron from an Indian Cavalry regiment, in Sherman tanks, was placed in support.

On the morning of 8 April the Battalion, mounted in its motley collection of wheeled vehicles, approached the Point 900 feature from the north-west. The armoured squadron swept on to the hill and reported by radio that there was a company plus of Japs holding the hill who "appeared to be willing to surrender". On what basis they had made this rather enigmatic assumption Dodgy Som Dutt could not discover, because the squadron, instead of dominating the hill until we could arrive, "swanned" off, apparently on some other mission, in rather cavalier style. With the Japs virtually without anti-tank mines or anti-tank guns, the armour could afford to be bold, whereas we infantry in soft-skinned vehicles and on our feet could not afford to jeopardize our men's lives with unnecessary risks.

Dodgy wisely decided that, despite this information, it would be most risky to attempt to drive on to Point 900 in our vehicles, since there was certainly no white flag showing from the top. We debussed and he ordered a quick advance on foot, two companies forward, my B Company on the left and D Company (Joe Hudson) on the right, followed by Battalion HQ with the two other rifle companies in reserve. Orders were to disarm the Japs, take them prisoner and then dig in on the top. We and D Company set off in a properly dispersed assault formation up the hill. Soon after we set off my company was engaged by a single isolated LMG post on my left flank. I sent a section to stalk and destroy the post, but they ran away.

As we advanced up the hill we caught sight of the odd Jap, but they did not open fire. Just below the summit there was a nullah running at right angles across our front, very like the deep ditches which are found around the summit of ancient hill-works in England. I was feeling wary, almost to the point of apprehension at this unusual circumstance, and I could feel the tension in all the men around me. We simply had no real idea whether the Japs did intend to surrender or whether we were advancing into a dangerous trap. Everyone was poised to take immediate counter-action if the latter were the case.

I was up with the leading right-hand platoon and just behind the line of the leading section. We were on the crest of the slope before it dipped down into the nullah/ditch, just below the final summit when suddenly there was one rifle shot and a sepoy just a few paces in front of me was lifted into the air, about a foot, and then crashed down dead. He had been fired on by a Jap from the bottom of the ditch as he was silhouetted on the skyline.

This was one dead sepoy too many for B Company who dropped any idea of taking prisoners and simply went fighting mad. I shouted at them to take prisoners, but they were heedless and Subedar Moghal Baz, my 2IC, cried out, "It is no good, sahib! They won't listen". In fact they were in a blood lust, the only time I have ever seen men in one, and a terrible and awesome thing it was to witness. They were baying in high-pitched screams, with their lips drawn back over their teeth which gave them a ghastly wolflike insane grin. I found myself both exhilarated and appalled by this sheer animal lust to kill. In about ten minutes of grenade work, tommy and Bren-gun fire and the bayonet the whole Jap company was wiped out, with no prisoners taken. They put up little resistance and I only had one other man killed. At one stage I saw a Jap officer, the company commander as it turned out, scurrying away over a mound. I was standing by one of the best Bren gunners in the company and gave him a quick order to kill my opposing number; the Bren gunner promptly put a burst through the Jap. It was the only time in the war that I ever saw a Jap officer running away. The Company later presented me with his sword, which I have kept to this day.

Joe Hudson's company on our right had successfully taken over an enemy platoon position further along the same feature, which was too far away for us to consolidate on a two-company position, and so my company dug in on the top of Point 900. The Jap dead, numbering 124, were all dumped in the nullah and left there.

The war in Burma was fought with a savagery that did not happen in campaigns in the Western Desert, Italy or North-West Europe, though it certainly did in the fighting between the Germans and Russians in Russia. Thus, throughout the Burma Campaign, I never once recall burying Jap dead. If there were sappers about, and there were when we captured Meiktila, the large number of Jap dead were simply bulldozed into pits. Otherwise we just shoved them into nullahs, or well away from our positions, for the jackals and vultures to dispose of. This was not quite as callous as it might appear. There is one Indian sect, the Parsis, whose dead are deliberately fed to vultures as part of their funeral rites, in Towers of Silence. These are circular brick towers about seventy feet or so high, with a metal grid at the top and the south-facing quadrant of the tower open at the bottom. Corpses are placed on the grid where the vultures eat all their flesh; the skeletons gradually crumble in the hot sun and fall to the bottom, where the sun finally turns them into dust, which is dispersed by the wind. Indians, other than Parsis, were of course aware of this method of disposing of dead, and so did not view it with the abhorrence that westerners might.

At dusk that evening, as we stood to, the euphoria had completely evaporated to be replaced, in my case and that of Moghal Baz, by a deep melancholy. He was a Pathan, from one of the hardest races on earth and a seasoned soldier, but he clearly voiced the feeling of many of us, when he said to me, as we gazed down on the horror of that nullah, "Even the Japs are human beings".

Down the years I have often pondered that battle. It was certainly not an encounter in which I can take much pride. My conscience is clear, since I have never been in any doubt that the Japs opened fire first, killing one of my men, and that we were therefore fully justified in killing them before they could kill any more of us. All the same I wish that it had happened differently. A key factor was undoubtedly the somewhat precipitate departure of the armour; had they remained until we arrived, it would probably never have happened as it did.

I have tried to analyse what the Japs' real intention was. Judging by the poor standard of their defences, their failure to fight back and the cowardice of their commander, I am sure that they were either second-grade infantry or even a scratch force sent out to block a thrust by us from the west. They probably did intend to surrender under the overwhelming strength of a squadron of Sherman tanks. The fact that they did not fire on us as we were climbing up the hill supports this theory. Once the tanks had gone, there may have been a change of mind by at least some of them. Under a weak commander these doubters may have been tempted to ignore the order to surrender and to fight back. The Jap soldier who did open fire may have thought so and, when a tempting target presented itself, he fired. Alternatively it may have been a nervous reaction to our proximity. We shall never know.

It would of course have been ideal if we could have avoided the awful slaughter and taken prisoners. However, the tension and fear of walking into a trap, as we climbed the hill, strained nerves to breaking point, and the killing of my one soldier released that tension in an orgy of killing. Though my conscience is clear, the outcome has always troubled me. It is a stark reminder of the sheer bloodiness of war.

Chapter 13

The Second Shot

In April 1945 our Division was thrusting south on the main Mandalay-Rangoon road, hell-bent on capturing Rangoon, before, as actually happened, some other British forces picked it off like a ripe plum without any hard fighting, not least because our Division had been driven out of Rangoon and Burma some three years before and we were quite keen to balance up the record. Not surprisingly, therefore, our brigade commander had the whip out and we were pressing on hard, ignoring small parties of broken, disorganized Japs to the flanks. We were a motorized or mobile division, which, though commonplace in the Western Desert and Europe, was somewhat unusual in Burma. "Motorized" was perhaps too grandiloquent a phrase for simply saying that every battalion had enough of its own transport to move itself on wheels. The "wheels" were a motley collection of British and American army vehicles in the three- or four-ton range. We had started off from Imphal nearly a thousand miles away, in February, and by now many of the original vehicles had broken down. My company's "wheels" were therefore reduced in numbers and my men were jam-packed in with no space of any sort.

One day as we were advancing south, but in reserve, a radio message came from Dodgy to pull off the road to allow two batteries of guns to go through; my company was directed to a small Burmese village about a quarter of a mile away to the left of the axis of the road.

We pulled off to the village. By now, after years of fighting and many weeks of mobile advance, we had our laager drill worked out

– central point, leading platoon one hundred and twenty degrees sector left; second platoon one hundred and twenty degrees sector right; third platoon filling the remaining one hundred and twenty degrees sector in rear and company headquarters in the middle. On arrival in this particular village we thus deployed and all the usual quiet, relaxed but efficient battle drill of seasoned troops took place – a quick comb through the village for Japanese; sentries put out with Bren guns; "cam" (camouflage) up the vehicles, against at this stage a negligible risk of enemy air attack; the usual personal reliefs of a "comfort stop" and a good brew up.

As I pulled into the centre of the village in my jeep, with the company headquarter vehicle behind, I noticed, in a clearing between some huts, a small group of Burmese men grouped round a figure lying on the ground, apparently being given first aid. Accompanied by my "shadow", a crack tommy gunner, and my second in command Subedar Moghal Baz, I strolled over towards this group, more out of idle curiosity and a desire to stretch cramped legs than any serious military intention. We were met by a chilling sight. Lying on the ground was a diseased and very badly wounded Japanese soldier, his left leg was completely shattered, bloated and stinking of gangrene, and he was very clearly dying. The Burmese, far from ministering any succour, were watching one of their number push a long sharpened bamboo stick as far up the Jap's anal passage as he possibly could, obviously for the sheer perverted pleasure of inflicting cruelty. Even despite the appalling nature of his wounds, the dying Jap was moaning in agony from this torture.

Our attitude to the Japanese then (and as far as I personally am concerned it has not changed – but see Appx C) was an ambivalent one; we could not but admire them for their courage, their fanatical sense of duty and their stoical acceptance of hardship. We despised them for the way that, as a deliberate policy, not isolated acts of indiscipline, they stained the honour of their army by their treatment of civilians and prisoners of war, and not least because, three years earlier when they had overrun our battalion, they had deliberately butchered all our walking wounded and slightly wounded regardless. Therefore, in the heat of battle we killed them (and in the final stages of the Burma campaign, killed them in considerable numbers) as they had killed us. And yet, after the

71

frenzy of battle had subsided, that strange compassion which often occurs between front-line troops of opposing armies for the poor "so and so" on the other side, suffering all the same fears and hardships, often took over. The very few prisoners of war, especially wounded ones that allowed themselves to be captured, were treated, even by such hard men as Pathans, with surprising kindness. The idea of deliberately torturing a helpless enemy was anathema and would have been regarded as a clear breach of the Indian soldier's code of honour, of "izzat", about which Philip Mason has written so eloquently in his book *A Matter Of Honour*.

As we drew closer to this nasty little group, all but the torturer himself drew back and stood looking at me with understandable apprehension. The torturer himself was so utterly absorbed in his terrible pleasures that he did not at first see us. No one who has been to war is short of the sight of horrors that he would prefer to forget, but the ghastly contorted smile of pleasure on that Burman's face haunts me to this day. Finally, even he somehow sensed a change in the atmosphere; he cocked his head sideways away from the Jap and saw an unfamiliar pair of boots and jungle green trousers. Slowly he got up and turned to face me and to look me in the eyes. He did not like what he saw there.

Half an hour later the guns had passed through and we were on the move again. Before we left there had been two shots: one, the *coup de grâce* for the dying Japanese soldier for whom we could clearly do nothing, except a quick clean soldier's death, since we certainly could not leave him to be tortured to death; the other was an unsoldierly accidental discharge. Or was it?

Chapter 14

A Quid Pro Quo

Historically Pathans are one of the world's great fighting races and, in their homeland on the old North-West Frontier and in southern Afghanistan, extremely formidable, as the British, and more recently the Russians, have discovered to their cost.

As a professional soldier, the Pathan was an enigmatic prospect. Up to the First World War, the Baluch Regiment recruited from the tribal areas, which were not directly under British rule – Mahsuds from Waziristan and Afridis from the Khyber Pass and from the Tirah to its west. After 1918 this policy changed and only Pathans from British-administered India were recruited in the four regiments, out of nineteen, enlisting them in the infantry of the Indian Army. The Baluchis recruited Khattaks from around Kohat and Yusufzais from the area east of the Khyber around Mardan.

Of all the martial races recruited in the Indian Army the mercurial Pathans' efficacy as a soldier depended most on the quality of leadership. In the Retreat from Burma, with the loss of officers and VCOs whom they knew, our Pathan company's morale had faltered badly. Pat Lindsay, with his vast experience of Indian soldiers, realizing this, had, while the battalion was being rebuilt in 1942/43, put the Pathan company under Siri, who, though a Hindu, was a proven company commander of great personal bravery and an excellent trainer of soldiers. This policy had paid off and in all the heavy fighting in the Chin Hills and in the Battle of Imphal the Pathans had fought very well indeed.

Advice given by old hands to young officers first put in command of Pathans usually followed the line: "Work them hard from dawn

73

to dusk on good soldierly work, ideally involving weapon handling; send them to bed with a really good meal; be rock firm and scrupulously fair in all your dealings and laugh with them a lot, and you won't have much trouble". Certainly after two years as Adjutant to be given command of a company of Pathans, as I was privileged to do in the latter stages of the Battle of Imphal, was a marvellous experience, with seldom a dull moment and quite a few highly diverting ones.

One of the main, if not the greatest, desires of a Pathan, be he a soldier of the Sarkar (i.e. Government of India – the term "Raj" was seldom used in those days) or a tribesman on the Frontier, was to possess his own private weapon. For obvious reasons the possession of firearms was strictly controlled by the Government of the North-West Frontier Province. However once the war against the Japanese started in Burma, a trickle of weapons, British and Japanese, "lost and found" on the battlefield, began to find its way to the Frontier. From time to time general, divisional and battalion orders contained exhortations against this flow, inspired by government. Despite dire threats of courts martial no one took much notice. We felt, perhaps a little arrogantly, that we had other more urgent preoccupations than the worries of some ICS wallah two thousand miles away in what seemed from the Assam/Burma border, a cushy billet.

In October 1944 our battalion, having fought throughout the Battle of Imphal, was, with the rest of the division out of the line in Eastern India, charging up its batteries and training hard for the final offensive against the Japanese in Burma in 1945.

Early one day, as I was shaving in my tent, I was called to the phone by Roderick Maclean, the Adjutant, who told me that there was to be a snap check of all sub-units composed of Pathans, of which there were only two in the whole division: my company and one from a battalion of the Frontier Force Regiment. Maurice Wright required me to cancel my training programme for the day, send the whole company out for a route march under my company 2IC, whilst I personally went through the kit of every man in the company, assisted by a small team of reliable NCOs, to see if any weapons were being held illegally. Now of all the distasteful jobs that an officer can be landed with, searching the kit of his men must be very high. The British private soldier or Indian Sepoy had little he could call his own, and no privacy. However, in his locker in barracks or kit bag/pack on active service were those few personal, private, secret parts of his life that most men have. Searching my men's kit would be rather like peeping through keyholes. Moreover, our division had a high proportion of Gurkha battalions and staff officers from Gurkha regiments, who as a result of innumerable Frontier encounters did not like Pathans! I protested strongly, with some "bolshy" counter-suggestions about "bloody" Gurkhas and how about the brigade and divisional staff coming to do their own dirty work. Roderick diplomatically let me bang on for a bit and expressed his sympathy, but insisted that regrettably it had to be done, and would I please be kind enough to let him have a report by noon.

My company 2IC was a marvellous man, Subedar Moghal Baz MC, a Yusufzai from that great fighting tribe of Pathans. Not very tall but immensely broad and powerful, hardened by fighting on the Frontier and the earlier fighting in Burma, and brave to a fault, he was a tower of strength. I told him that the day's training programme was cancelled and he was to take the company off for a route march returning not before 11 a.m., leaving Naiks (corporals) X Y and Z behind. I gave no explanation for this, but he accepted the change in the planned day's training programme with a cheerful grin and in due course the company slogged off, leaving me to my searching.

I have only had to search my men's kit twice, once on this occasion and once subsequently in my British Regiment. Apart from the aforementioned distastefulness, it is also very revealing. Imagine for a moment what you would keep of your possessions spread around your home, if all you could have was what you could carry in your pack or kitbag, in addition to all your military gear – not much really and therefore of some importance. It is not too fanciful to say that what one found was in many ways a true revelation of the man's inner life, and it produced some surprises: the apparently ordinary, decent man with the really nasty pictures or books; the "hard case" with pictures, obviously treasured, of a happy wife and children or of parents; perhaps the most revealing and saddest, of all, the man with absolutely nothing personal of any kind. So I set about the dreary business, helped by the three Naiks. We established a drill: one Naik opened up a kitbag and laid out the kit; I then went through it, while he opened another; the other Naiks meanwhile packed up the kit I had just searched. I then went through everyone's bedding. Perhaps surprisingly, at least to me, I came across no weapons; there were a couple of water bottles which seemed to weigh rather heavily and which proved to be full of small arms ammunition. I had just dismissed the Naiks when I remembered that I had been asked to examine all kit, and so, merely in a spirit of pious obedience to orders, I went also to Subedar Moghal Baz's tent and casually searched his cupboard and bed. To my surprise, and then concern, beneath the mattress was a British service revolver. My first thought, or perhaps hope, was that he had drawn it out of the company arms kote (armoury) for cleaning and failed to return it, naughty but not very serious. I locked the revolver away in a tin box in my tent and then went off to check the company arms register. No such numbered revolver was on charge to my company!

I was tempted to seek Maurice Wright's advice "off the record", but in the end rejected it. It seemed rather wet to offload what I regarded as my command problem on him. I also had an uneasy feeling that he would go "by the book". I therefore took the plunge. I rang Roderick and told him that I had searched every kit, had found two water bottles full of ammunition whose owners I proposed to deal with at my next company orders, and "had nothing more to report". I chose the last phrase with care so that I did not lie, though I had put my own head in the noose by saying that I had (chosen to decide that I had) nothing more to report.

The company returned. I called for Subedar Moghal Baz and told him what my orders had been and why he had had to take the company for a march; that I had found two water bottles full of ammunition and that I had reported this, but nothing else, to Battalion Headquarters. I made no mention of the discovery of a revolver in his bed. He looked me straight in the eye; gave the usual acknowledgement "*Achi Bat, Sahib*", saluted and went away. I gave him full marks for sang-froid and coolness under fire (he was even cooler under real fire) since he must have wondered in that second, before I told him that I had reported nothing, that his whole career and honour had been at stake. Though he and I served together for another year and a half through all the fighting in the reconquest of Burma and came to know each other very well, no mention of this incident was ever made.

All day I wondered what I was going to do with the revolver. After dinner in the mess tent, and a couple of extra whiskies, I went to my tent, unlocked the box, took out the offending revolver and walked out into the beautiful, starlit night of the Indian cold weather, to a small jheel (reservoir) about a quarter of a mile away and hurled the revolver as far as I could into it. Brought up on the Arthurian legends, I half-expected to see a hand come out of the water to collect it!

Early in 1945 the battalion went back into Burma and the following April, after much fighting, we were pressing south on the road to Rangoon, hoping to capture it before the monsoon began. Our division was held up north of Pegu, a large town where the Japs were holding positions on hills covered with thick jungle. The battalion, now under Dodgy Som Dutt, was ordered to capture them and we put in an attack with my company on the left and Clifford Martin (A Coy) on the right. We managed to capture the summit, but any attempt to exploit through the objective was met by heavy machine-gun fire from hidden reverse positions beyond the objective. It was too thick for tanks and the gunners had crest-clearance problems. During the day I had quite a few casualties, including both my forward right platoon commander and gunner Forward Observation Officer killed, and my company officer Tony Davies wounded. Subedar Moghal Baz was, as always, a tower of strength. As dusk settled it appeared that the Japanese were about to counter-attack with tanks and we continued digging in hard. At that moment one of my forward platoon sent in a Jap prisoner of war. As I thought it important to get him back via Battalion Headquarters to Brigade Headquarters, where a Japanese-speaking interrogator might get some useful information about the strength of the enemy facing me, I decided to send him back quickly. Being still under mortar fire, I ordered that he should be blindfolded, in case he got away in the jungle if the fire got too heavy. However, the prisoner thought that the blindfolding was a prelude to being shot and struggled madly until three men's combined efforts got him to the ground. At that moment a sepoy, from the reserve platoon section located near Company Headquarters, who I had noticed during the day had been conspicuously windy, went over and kicked the prisoner in the face. I had had a very hard day's fighting, which did not look as if it was by any means over, and something snapped in my own self-control. I went over to the cowardly sepoy, struck him hard in the face and shouted out, "You coward, to kick a defenceless man when you have been skulking in your trench all day". Officers in the Indian Army simply did not hit their men on any pretext and I was absolutely wrong to do so, however much the provocation in the stress of battle. I spent a thoroughly miserable night, first dealing with the threatened counter-attack, which was fortunately broken up by some impressive artillery defensive fire, and secondly brooding on the likely outcome of my loss of control. We patrolled vigorously throughout the night and shortly before dawn the Japs facing us pulled out and the whole feature was therefore clear of enemy. Nevertheless my morale was low. I could not believe that news of my striking a soldier would not somehow get back to the ears of my commanding officer, that I would be relieved of my command and probably court-martialled.

I was indeed called back to Battalion Headquarters. Before I went an odd thing happened. The erring sepoy came to me and apologized to me for his act of cowardice, shedding an interesting light on the concept of honour of the Indian soldier, which put cowardly behaviour far higher in the scale of military wrong than mere assault. At Battalion Headquarters Dodgy, basking in the recently received congratulations of the brigade and divisional commander on the success of the battalion's attack, was equally forthcoming in congratulating me and nothing was said about my error, neither then nor ever. I half-expected that Roderick Maclean, the Adjutant, might quietly take me aside and say that it was known but the Commanding Officer had officially taken no notice, but this too did not happen. I can only speculate as to why and I am pretty certain in my own mind that it was due to the influence of Subedar Moghal Baz on the men of my company. Certainly only someone of his stature and personality could have ensured that such an event remained sealed within the company. Perhaps he went round and said something to the effect that I was their officer to whom they owed their loyalty, that the sepoy deserved it and that any breach of what must be a secret to be held within the company would be dealt with by him as a personal matter with all the undertones of a Pathan blood feud. Suffice to say that it never did. A quid pro quo indeed.

In thirty-six years of soldiering, I collected my fair share of rockets, mostly richly deserved. Along the way I did get a few "strawberries", mostly due to good luck rather than good judgement. The one that I cherish most concerns Moghal Baz. During the Burma fighting I was seldom able, for operational reasons, to feed at Battalion Headquarters and so decided to eat Indian food, and it was my practice, unless actually under fire, always to have my evening meal with him. We would discuss the past day's events, the prospects of the morrow and then philosophize about soldiering and life in general. One such evening, suddenly, out of the blue he said to me, "I would like you to know, Sahib, that with you I have served with great 'izzat' (honour)". From him and knowing the significance of his "izzat" to the Indian fighting man, I took immense pride in this – and still do.

Thirty-one years later Clifford Martin and I had the pleasure of accepting an invitation from our old regiment to visit them as their guests on the North-West Frontier. Among the many privileges and kindnesses shown to us was the opportunity to go and see Moghal Baz at his home in his village some miles north of Mardan. In the intervening years he had fulfilled one of his life's ambitions as a devout Muslim, to do the Pilgrimage (Haj) to Mecca. Now a very old bearded man, he nevertheless retained his memory and great sense of humour, and we had an absorbing meal, sitting out in the warm winter sunshine with the distant snows on the Malakand as a background. We talked much about "the old days" and I was tempted to bring these two linked incidents into the conversation. Prudently, on subsequent reflection, I did not; old secrets, like old soldiers, should just fade away.

F. Background Events

May–September 1945

After the recapture of Rangoon on 2 May 1945, 17th Indian Division moved north and was strung out along the main Rangoon–Toungoo road, dealing with the remnants of the Japanese 28th Army trapped by the rapid British advance. In August 1945 our Brigade took over positions on the west bank of the Sittang, east of Pegu. We were 'in the line' on VJ (Victory over Japan) Day, some fifty to sixty miles from where we had began the Burma Campaign in January 1942.

Chapter 15

Zan, Zar, Zamin –
(Women, Gold, Land)
– A Story Of Murder

Compared with officers in the British Army, officers of the Indian Army did not have to deal with many domestic welfare cases of their men. The strong and widely based family structure of the Indian ensured that family problems which, in the British Army would involve SSAFA and other welfare organizations, were often handled within the family sphere. If this failed, then disputes were often settled by the Indian Civil Service Collector or District Commissioner, either as a result of a direct petition by the family concerned, or as the result of a case put up by the sepoy on his family's behalf, through his company commander, who in turn forwarded it to the appropriate ICS official. The advice on welfare matters often given to a young officer in the Indian Army by his elders was that "Zan, Zar, Zamin" (Women, Gold, Land), either separately or collectively, would be the background of every welfare case that he encountered.

The true motive for the murder is obscure and there were, and remain, at least two conjectures. It certainly never came out at the trial, and I prefer to believe that it was a story of "Zan", or, if you prefer it, the occidental *"Cherchez la femme"*. It went back to events at the Regimental Centre in the palmy days of peace before the War. There a young and promising Punjabi Mussulman lance naik, let us call him Khan Bahadur, had his young wife apparently in the official Married Lines. Even in the more relaxed attitudes of the late twentieth century, Muslims have very strong views about the sanctity and reputation of their womenfolk; back in the thirties and forties this was no less strong and in many cases, certainly amongst Punjabi Mussulmans and Pathans, fanatically observed. Married women were hidden behind the strict taboos of the zenana and the chador. Also at the Regimental Centre at that time was an older and more senior havildar, let us call him Mahbub Khan. He was married also, but his wife observed the more customary practice of being at his home in the Punjab. Somehow or other Lance Naik Khan Bahadur came to believe that Havildar Mahbub Khan had been involved in some incident which reflected on the honour and reputation of his, Khan Bahadur's, wife. Whether this was true or even plausible, given the strict isolation of wives, may never be known; probably not. The crucially important factor however was that Khan Bahadur believed it to be true, and the thought festered deep in his mind.

The war came and Khan Bahadur and Mahbub Khan went their separate ways to different battalions and different theatres of the war. In 1945, in the closing stages of the war in Burma, fate decreed that they should both be posted as reinforcements to the 7th battalion in Burma – Khan Bahadur, now as a Company Havildar Major and Mahbub Khan as the Subedar Major, the most senior Indian officer of the battalion. That there was bad blood between them was apparently known to some in the battalion, but the extent of that knowledge was never entirely clear. As neither were in my company, I certainly knew nothing of it.

In July of that year, at the height of the monsoon and following the capture of Rangoon, our division was strung out along the main Rangoon-Mandalay road, about 100 miles north of Rangoon in strong defended bastions. Our task was to destroy the Japanese 28th Army which had been cut off in the Arakan and west of the Irrawaddy valley by the speed of our capture of Rangoon, and which was now attempting to escape eastward, firstly across the Irrawaddy valley, then across the low mountain range of the Pegu Yomas, then across the main Rangoon-Mandalay road and finally across the Sittang River, which was held by their main army on the eastern bank. Because of the monsoon our only quick method of movement was along the main road, but companies, either singly or in greater strength, supported by guns, tanks and machine guns, engaged the Japs from these secure bases and also mounted offensive patrols to seek out and destroy them. At that time D Company and my B Company were in such a bastion with Battalion Headquarters inside our perimeter. Whilst I and D Company Commander operated quite separately outside the perimeter, I was made responsible for the overall local defence of the two company/Battalion Headquarter bastion. Because of the monsoon and the low offensive spirit of the Japs all but our sentries were able to sleep in Burmese buildings and bashas (bamboo huts) in order to get some shelter from the almost continuous rain. Slit trenches permanently filled with water and so defensive works had to be built up with sandbags.

One night I was woken by an explosion and, hearing the call "Stand To", obviously expected some sort of Jap activity. However, it soon became clear from my sentries that the explosion had come from within our position in the general area of Battalion Headquarters. I set out with a torch toward the sound of the explosion and soon found one or two sepoys gathered outside the basha where Subedar Major Mahbub Khan slept. Inside I saw his body lying on a camp bed, clearly shattered by a grenade which had exploded underneath it. He simply was not the man for suicide and, even if he had been, he would have hardly put the grenade under his bed, so it was clearly a case of murder. After three and a half years fighting in Burma I had seen the death of soldiers and civilians in every conceivable form of horror, and considered myself pretty well immune to shock, but the sight of this fine man, murdered in his sleep, gave me a very real chill of horror and revulsion.

I immediately informed both Roderick Maclean and the Regimental Medical officer at Battalion Headquarters and got in touch with Joe Hudson, commanding D Company, my own 2IC and Tommy Bruin, the Intelligence Officer, who was responsible for Battalion Headquarters personnel, and ordered a general "Stand To" and a check of all grenades. This measure was a somewhat faint hope because in Burma once ammunition of any sort was issued to rifle companies they ceased to be accountable for them in the same sense that one accounted for ammunition and explosives in peacetime. However, it was worth the try and so the rainy night was disturbed by much subdued orders and activity by a lot of sleepy soldiers. Suddenly there was the sound of a single shot from the direction of D Company and some five minutes later Joe Hudson sent a message to say that there had been an accidental discharge of his weapon, a rifle, by Company Havildar Major Khan Bahadur who was being sent to the battalion RAP (Regimental Aid Post) with a nasty flesh wound in his arm. There the Medical Officer, pre-occupied with examining Mahbub Khan's body by the light of a hurricane bhutti (lamp), put a dressing on the wound and, taking Khan Bahadur at his word, wrote "GSW" (gun shot wound) on the medical card, always tied to a casualty, sent him off to the Field Ambulance, which was inside our bastion. I remember being mildly surprised at this news. We had been fighting a long time in Burma and, to use that old-fashioned phrase, were well-seasoned troops with a high standard of battle discipline. Accidental discharges of weapons were a rare occurrence, certainly from such a senior soldier as a Company Havildar Major. No traceable loss of a grenade having been reported to me, I repeated them to the CO who in turn ordered a general stand down, and we all got our heads down for the remainder of the night. Meanwhile Mahbub Khan's body had been removed to the Field Ambulance.

My own personal involvement in the case ceased from thereon and I simply became a sad observer of the subsequent events. Next morning there were two major developments. Our MTO (Motor Transport Officer), "Fish" Herring, who rather fancied himself – and, as things turned out, with some justification – as an amateur detective, at the normal pre-dawn Stand To examined the area of the murder in the half-light and noticed an intermittent, but clear blood trail leading from the Subedar Major's basha towards D Company. Reported to Battalion Headquarters, this led the CO and the Adjutant to the conclusion that Company Havildar Major Khan Bahadur must be a strong suspect. At that time there were two types of fuses for our "36" hand grenades – a "four-second" for throwing by hand and in close-quarter fighting – and a "seven-second" for firing from a cup discharger screwed on to a rifle and propelled by a ballistite cartridge. This latter technique had been used in the trench warfare of the 1914/18 War but had rather gone out of fashion in the Second World War, except for the firing of smoke grenades, with their high phosphorous content, for setting fire to jungle and buildings in order to flush out the Japs; so some seven second fuses were still held. The inference was that he intended to use a seven-second-fused grenade for the murder, had mistakenly used a four-second one and had not got out of range quickly enough. Realizing that a small grenade flesh wound would make him a suspect, he attempted to cover up his grenade wound by firing his rifle into the air, but significantly, not through the grenade wound in his arm, either because he funked it or because it was not physically possible to pull the trigger of his rifle when the barrel was pointing at his wound.

Secondly, the duty Medical Officer at the Field Ambulance, an experienced doctor, who had been the battalion's MO and who was a man of complete integrity, examined Khan Bahadur's wound and, seeing that it was not a bullet wound but a fragment wound, altered the diagnosis to "Grenade Wound".

The whole process of military law then went into play: court of enquiry, summary of evidence, and in due course Khan Bahadur was arraigned by general court martial on a charge of murder. The next senior and suitable Viceroy's Commissioned officer in the battalion, another Punjabi Mussulman (let us call him Riasat Khan), was made acting Subedar Major and later permanently confirmed in the appointment.

The question in due course arose as to who was to be appointed, in accordance with Khan Bahadur's wishes, as his defending officer. I had previously been Adjutant of the battalion and had thereby acquired a reputation, not really justified, of having a good knowledge of the Indian Army military code and I was warned that there was a strong possibility that I might be asked to defend him. This gave me food for much troubled thought. On the one hand I was convinced that Khan Bahadur was guilty and that "Grenade Wound" was the correct diagnosis. On the other hand, as his Defending Officer I would have had the moral duty of doing my best for him, particularly where his life was at stake. The only piece of evidence linking him to the murder was the grenade wound. Did my moral duty extend to raising doubts about the change of diagnosis or even to imputing a stitch-up of the evidence to secure a conviction? I could then have argued in court that, where the death penalty was involved, they had to be absolutely sure and, if there was any doubt, to acquit him. Khan Bahadur in the end asked for and was given the services of an Indian Officer in another regiment who had legal training. The latter did his best (though it did not include any reference to the change in diagnosis), but Khan Bahadur, still not admitting his guilt, was found guilty of murder and sentenced to be hanged. In due course he went to his death in Moulmein Jail with courage and dignity. It fell to my company of Pathans, fellow Muslims, to do the death watch. I got the distinct impression that in their view sacrificing his life to avenge a personal dishonour more than compensated for his cowardly method of achieving it.

Throughout the time of his arrest and trial a very ugly story came confidentially to my notice from other British officers in the Battalion. Its substance was that Subedar Major Riasat Khan had, with machiavellian guile, treacherously engineered the whole thing so that he could get the coveted promotion. The story was that for weeks on end he had been feeding Khan Bahadur's mind with poison about the dishonour that the murdered man had caused him, all those years ago, and that the front line circumstances now gave him an easy chance to avenge his honour. I did not at first give much credence to it, if only because I felt sure that if the CO had had any doubts he would never have promoted Riasat Khan to Subedar Major. But later doubts formed in my mind. It was my practice to have my evening meal with my 2IC Moghal Baz. I was therefore considerably surprised one evening when he, one of the most fearless men I have ever met, told me that he deeply feared Subedar Major Riasat Khan. We were on somewhat thin ice here, because the normal unwritten military code did not really encourage British officers to discuss the Subedar Major with more junior VCOs. However, Moghal Baz and I had been through a lot together and this was an informal "off the record" discussion; and my curiosity perhaps overcame my good sense, so I asked him why. "Well," said Moghal Baz, "for one thing he speaks Pushtu." Now that may seem an extraordinary remark but in the context of the Indian Army understandable. Apparently Riasat Khan, a Punjabi Mussulman who of course spoke Urdu, the lingua franca of the Indian Army, and his native Punjabi, had learned Pushtu, the Pathan language, when employed in some intelligence appointment on the Frontier before the war. However, though a Welsh-speaking Englishman might cause some surprise "in the valleys", it would hardly be grounds for fear. Moghal Baz added that there were other things including the Khan Bahadur affair, then, perhaps realizing he was getting on to very dangerous ground, clammed up and I did not feel it prudent to press him. It made me think, however, of the earlier rumours and caused me to wonder. I certainly treated Subedar Major Riasat Khan with a very watchful eye for the remainder of my time in the battalion, even though I had always liked him and got on with him.

Perhaps *"Zan, Zar, Zamin"* is not an apt title for this story and that Kipling's often-quoted "For four things greater than all things are, Women and Horses and Power and War" is nearer the truth, if, in my case, you leave out the horses, though there are of course many who would include them. Personally I would go for dogs, preferably white bull-terriers, but that is another story.

Chapter 16

A Sad Story

This is a story of the impact of two widely differing subjects – the attitude of Indian soldiers to their officers and homosexuality.

In a good British Regiment the loyalty of the men, both individually and collectively, is never in doubt. Obviously some officers command more respect and loyalty than others, but that is always tempered with British common sense: good officers are liked and respected, but very seldom put on pedestals. The Indian soldier often did just that. The British have often been accused of ruling India on a colour bias; in fact, in my view, they merely adapted their own class system to the Hindu caste system. Whilst this did not apply in a religious way among Muslims, they too had a clearly defined social order and, contrary to popular belief, every white man in India was not a "sahib"; there were too many ordinary British soldiers about. The Indian soldier perceived that British Society (then) contained a ruling class – the sahib, his officers – and a lower class from which British soldiers were drawn – the "gora" or white face. The Indian soldier therefore put his officers in a special category and, though this was all very flattering, it did take some living up to, to be a "pukka sahib", a "proper chap". They were generally far less critical of their officers than British soldiers and would regard eccentricities with good humour. However, once a British officer had failed in that style in which the Indian soldier regarded the "pukka sahib" should behave, then he was finished, utterly and completely.

To say that homosexuality did not exist in the Indian Army would be as unwise as to say that it did not exist in the British

Army, but it existed on a minuscule scale and was very rarely a problem which affected good order or military discipline. Some Indian races were regarded as having more such leanings than others. The practice certainly did exist amongst Pathans, as it often does seem to appear among wild and fanatical tribesmen, especially where female infanticide, on social-religious grounds, was not unknown. The famous Pathan marching song *Zakhmi Dil*, 'The Wounded Heart', contained explicit homosexual overtones.

In the British Army if an officer suspected homosexual practices within his unit or sub-unit, it would be his duty to take positive action to deal with it. The unwritten practice in the Indian Army was more oblique, even though it was regarded with equal disfavour. If a British officer actually caught two sepoys *in flagrante delicto* then he would have to take action, but he certainly did not go looking for it. The whole matter was handled by the wisdom and vast experience of the Indian officers, the VCOs, and they were, in their own way, very tough on offenders. It was a matter that was hardly ever discussed. Once I remember querying why, when we had to draft a sepoy to the Brigade or Divisional Defence Platoon, my Subedar had proposed one really very good Brengunner. "I just think, Sahib, that he would be better away from the Company". I was just about to ask why when the penny dropped.

In the summer of 1945, when the Battalion was dealing with the breakout of the Japanese Army trapped west of the Irrawaddy, a reinforcement subaltern arrived: let us call him John (his real name) and Lewisham (not his real name). He had been at the Officers' Training School at Bangalore a term before me and therefore was senior to me in substantive rank, and yet I was a temporary Major. He was posted to me as a Company Officer. Though nothing was said to me by Som Dutt, my CO, I had the distinct impression that Lewisham had come under a cloud. I, naively but wrongly, assumed that he had failed in battle and was "windy". It proved to be quite wrong.

I found John Lewisham to be a perfectly competent officer and, though we got on all right, I did not really like him. Among young officers, especially in war, a certain amount of bawdy, but heterosexual talk is understandable, and probably, from a psychological point of view, normal and healthy, but John Lewisham had a really unclean mind in a way which I found distasteful. However, whatever faults he had, being windy was not one of them, and, though we were not involved in any heavy fighting, I could not fault him as an officer in that respect.

Then occurred an incident which had no great significance for me at the time, but which I realized afterwards was indeed so. Units and sub-units of retreating Japs often blundered into our positions at night, not with the intention of attacking us, but trying to find a way through to the Sittang River to our east and to the safety of their own main forces east of that river. Our job was to intercept them and inflict the maximum number of casualties. A body of Japs, perhaps fifty or sixty strong, hit us one night and we stood to. Company Headquarters was in a cockroach-infested rice mill just a short distance behind my two forward platoons. As we stood to, I said to John Lewisham, "You go up to 12 Platoon, John, will you. I'm going to 10 Platoon," and we disappeared our separate ways into the night. A mixture of some excellent defensive fire from our guns, by fixed line firing from a platoon of a Medium Machine-Gun battalion attached to me, plus our own efforts, soon dealt with the Japs. I stood the Company down, returned to Company Headquarters, sent a signal report to Battalion Headquarters and turned in again. I took a little while to get to sleep and noticed that John Lewisham had not returned. I thought that he might well have stayed chatting with the Platoon over a mug of tea and thought it a good thing for him to get to know the men of the Company.

About a fortnight later we redeployed and my Company, together with another rifle company, formed a bastion with Battalion Headquarters. I was ordered to go away for a day and a night to act as President of a Court Martial of a sepoy in another Battalion and left John Lewisham in command of the Company, even though technically my 2IC, Subedar Moghal Baz, was.

Shortly after I returned, Moghal Baz came to me looking very sombre and obviously with something heavy weighing on his mind. The conversation started something on the lines:

"Sahib, you know me well."

"I do indeed, Subedar Sahib."

"You know that I would not lightly or without very good reason make a serious accusation against a British Officer."

"That is very true, Subedar Sahib."

Then it all came tumbling out. John Lewisham had been making homosexual advances to sepoys, getting into their slit trenches, for example, and trying to fumble them. This had caused immense anger among the men and there was a plot afoot to shoot him.

My first reaction was of red-hot anger against John Lewisham's conduct. Whilst I have always personally viewed homosexuality with distaste, I am not homophobic and recognize that to some it is a natural state and not just an acquired vice.

If John had gone to some bumboy in a Burmese town bazaar to indulge himself I would have felt contempt, but I could have accepted it. To abuse his authority, position and prestige as a British Officer was, to me, unforgivable and I almost went and shot him myself. I cooled down and common sense fortunately took over. This was clearly not a situation that I could possibly handle at my level. The repercussions for the reputation and well-being of the whole battalion, if he were shot by the men, were too serious. I could not trust myself to confront John Lewisham with an accusation and, as I had such absolute confidence in Moghal Baz's integrity that I never doubted for one moment the truth of his report, I took him straight to Som Dutt to repeat his report. Although the latter was not always very decisive, on this occasion he did act with commendable speed and went straight off to the Brigade Commander, who also grasped the nettle.

I was ordered to put Lewisham under arrest in a secluded area and to put a guard of senior and trustworthy NCOs on him. He would then be shipped out the next day to some airfield and flown to India.

I spent an anxious night wondering if there would be some incident, but discipline held, and Lewisham disappeared the next day to ignominious oblivion. My company shrugged the whole thing off and it was soon forgotten – there was more fighting and eventful days to concern us all.

I sometimes wonder what happened to Lewisham. Nowadays, *autre temps, autre moeurs*!

Chapter 17

The Girls

In July 1945 my Pathan Company of the 7th/10th Baluchis was dug in on a redoubt centred on a cockroach-infested rice mill near the village of Kyauktaga on the main Rangoon–Pegu-Toungoo road in Central Burma. Our task was to deal with groups of Japanese soldiers from their 28th Army endeavouring to break out from the Pegu Yomas to our west, across the main road and then across the Sittang River to our east to the safety of the east bank, held by their main army. This involved rigorous patrolling to identify such enemy bodies and destroy them, both by our own resources, supported by our gunners, and by calling for air strikes.

One morning just after we had stood down from the dawn stand-to, I was having a restorative mug of char and shaving when I heard a lot of hearty laughter and Pushtu wisecracking going on outside. I sent my orderly to find out what was going on and he returned shortly afterwards grinning all over his face with the news that one of our patrols had captured some women who the patrol commander was now parading outside for my inspection. Pathan leg-pulling before breakfast did not always put me at my best and I went outside, not perhaps in the best of humour. To my surprise there indeed was the patrol commander, also grinning widely, with six Japanese comfort girls lined up demurely for my inspection.

Surprisingly, considering the monsoon conditions and the appalling state under which the Japanese were withdrawing, these girls looked very clean, tidy and cheerful, and not unattractive. Each girl was carrying a small cheap cardboard suitcase, which I got them to open; they all contained the same – hundreds of

Japanese Burma "banana" money notes and a spare pair of knickers. I ordered my Company Havildar Major to see that they were given food and drink and then put somewhere in the rice mill under guard. I then sent a signal to Battalion HQ on the lines of "Have captured six tarts. Request disposal instructions". This provoked the response that it was a bit early in the morning for Randle humour. I persisted and in the end got a signal to say that a party of military police would in due course come and collect them. Meanwhile my Pathans were enjoying themselves chatting up the girls, whom I began to suspect might be contemplating offering a bit of business. After all, the oldest profession is an all embracing one – literally. I was not, therefore, too unhappy when eventually a posse of redcaps did arrive and took the girls away, to the patronizing derision that all front-line troops, perhaps unfairly, tended in those days to regard military police.

That evening, over my customary meal with Moghal Baz, he remarked philosophically that it had been a unique day for him. "How so, Subedar Sahib?" I asked. "Sahib," he replied, "in all my service [and that included much hard fighting in Waziristan on the North-West Frontier, as well as Burma] I have never seen either women or military police in a front-line position. Today we have had both."

(*This tale originally appeared in the Newsletter of the Burma Campaign Fellowship Group and then, revised, in* Durbar, *the journal of the Indian Military Historical Society*).

Chapter 18

An *ad hoc* Elephant Battery

In June and July 1945 our division, the legendary 17th Indian, was strung out along the main Rangoon-Toungoo road in strongly fortified redoubts, dealing with the remnants of the Japanese 28th Army struggling to escape from the Pegu Yomas eastward to the safety of the east bank of the Sittang River.

About this time a new experimental heavy mortar, with mortar experts, arrived in the Division, with the task of carrying out trials as to the mortar's efficacy in the untried conditions of Burma. It was decided to carry out these trials in the paddy area between the Pegu Yomas and the main road. Additionally, some military genius decided that elephants would be a suitable porterage vehicle for carrying the mortar, there being a number of tame ex-forestry elephants and their Burmese mahouts available in the area. I, commanding the Pathan company of 7th/10th Baluchis, was detailed to provide the escort for this party. I was additionally tasked with the secondary and, as it turned out, wholly incompatible role of establishing my base in a good defensive position covering a likely exit from the Yomas, so that I could inflict maximum casualties on any Japanese parties emerging.

On the morning of our departure we immediately ran into difficulties. Elephants can pull enormous loads, but, surprisingly, as it turned out, they are not, for their size and strength, very good load carriers, not much better than big mountain artillery mules. The problem was exacerbated by the fact that these elephants had no experience or training in carrying loads, there was no proper equipment for lashing the mortar and ammunition, and the mortar

95

experts had done no test-loading. This considerably delayed our departure, with much exasperation by all concerned. We eventually arrived in the designated area and I sited my company in a good, well-camouflaged position covering the possible exit from the Yomas. It had been made clear to me that I was to ensure that the elephants were not shot up by any Japanese, so I had to keep them in or very near the perimeter of my position.

That was only the start of my problems. Firstly, elephants consume vast quantities of greenery and after a couple of days what had been a well-camouflaged position had been eaten bare by the voracious elephants and the position stuck out like a sore thumb. If I moved the position we would no longer be in a good tactical position to cover the likely exit from the Yomas. Secondly, elephants also produced vast quantities of dung, which, in the hot monsoon conditions, attracted equally vast numbers of flies and a hefty "pong". The Indian soldier, for religious and cultural reasons, was averse to handling any sort of excrement. The company sweeper insisted that he had enlisted to deal with human excrement, not elephant, and in any case he could not be expected to dig it down, because any hole soon filled up with monsoon water. I eventually persuaded my Pathans to agree to shift the dung out in the paddy, away from our position, on the grounds that they had so handled mule dung earlier in the war, when we had mules, and an elephant was a sort of big mule. It was not a happy business.

After a couple of days the mortar experts decided that it was time to test fire the mortar. They selected, as a firing position, a small mound rising above the sodden paddy. Although I had no responsibility for the trials, I decided to see how the test firing went. I went with the Observation Post (OP) party to a point several hundred yards forward of the base plate position, but well short of the planned impact area. The customary bedding-in rounds were ordered and we, in the OP position, stared ahead of us for the anticipated fall of shot. Off went the first bedding-in round, which dropped between the OP position and the base plate position! We went back to the base plate position to discover that the base plate had been driven about a foot into the sodden ground and was all at an angle. My interest in participating as a spectator in the trials abruptly ended!

After about a week my company was relieved, as originally

96

planned, by a company from 1st/10th Gurkhas commanded by an old friend, Tom Boyes. Eighteen months earlier we had both been adjutants of our respective battalions and leading lights in the "Adjutants' Union". He was not wildly excited by what he found. The sight of Gurkhas was always welcome in Burma, and to me their arrival had never been more so. Thereafter Tom and I always greeted each other with "How are the elephants?"

The Atom Bomb and the unexpected Japanese surrender put paid, as far as I can recall, to any introduction of the new mortar – just as well perhaps for the safety of our own troops.

Years later Tom and I were both living in the West Country and he and his wife came to a dinner party at our house. This anecdote went down very well with our other guests as the post-prandial port was circulated.

(*This story originally appeared in* Durbar, *the journal of the Indian Military Historical Society*).

Chapter 19

A Cruel Turn of Fate

It has been my experience that luck does play an enormous part in people's lives, both good and bad luck. Some men seem born lucky and, having the good sense to realize it, play it for all it is worth, often most successfully. Other lucky, often worthless, men get away with murder. Conversely, some men have only to commit just one blunder and pay for it, while others, fine men often, seem to be relentlessly, and through no fault of their own, pursued by misfortune after misfortune. This story, sadly, concerns a soldier in this latter category.

Badshah Gul was a Khattak Pathan from that fine Pathan tribe who live in the Kohat area of the North-West Frontier. Khattaks had bobbed hair, as did some Punjabi Mussulmen, which gave them at first glance, and to the ignorant, a slightly effeminate appearance, but they were a fine, soldierly race, expert players of the *surnai*, a sort of bagpipe, and renowned for the wildness of their Khattak dancing, very akin to Highland sword dances. (In 1938 the Baluch Regiment Pipes & Drums won the All-India Piping contest against stiff competition from several Scottish Regiments stationed in India.)

Badshah Gul, who had pre-war service on the Frontier, served in the Battalion throughout the whole Burma Campaign and was wounded during the Retreat in 1942. I came to know him well, first when he was Battalion Havildar Major (a responsible appointment, but nothing like as auspicious as the Regimental Sergeant Major of a British battalion) and I was Adjutant. He got promotion to Jemadar, did well and by the time I took command of the Pathan

Company he was commanding the Khattak Platoon as a Subedar. His two younger brothers were in the same platoon, a manning mistake in my view. He was not everyone's cup of tea; he had little sense of humour and tended to nag his men too much. His three great and compensating virtues were his courage, his exceptionally high sense of duty and his utter loyalty to the officer whom he was serving. I liked and admired him, despite his weak points.

At one stage in the fighting for the capture of Meiktila in March 1945 my company was ordered to carry out a company sweep to locate enemy dispositions. We ran into heavy opposition and Badshah Gul, with whose platoon I was advancing, was wounded a few paces from me. I got him under cover and he was safely evacuated to the RAP (Regimental Aid Post). He recovered and rejoined three months later. Shortly after he was wounded, one of his brothers a Naik (Corporal) Section Commander was also wounded and evacuated, and so I arranged for the third brother to be posted back to the Regimental Centre; it was asking too much of one family.

At the time of Badshah Gul's return, the Battalion was engaged in the so-called Battle of the Breakthrough, attempting to destroy those Japs endeavouring to get away to the east. Though we did not of course know it, the Hiroshima A-bomb was only days away. For some odd reason, the Battalion was issued with the PIAT (Projectile Infantry Anti-Tank). These had been in the Division for some time, but we had had no time to train with them.

Dodgy Som Dutt, the CO, ordered Tony Davies, my company officer, to do some live test firing, as he had some training in the use of the weapon, and Tony got Badshah Gul and some of his platoon to assist him. Tragically a projectile "cooked off" just after being fired. Badshah Gul was mortally wounded and Tony, for the second time in six months, slightly wounded.

Badshah Gul was evacuated to the Field Ambulance Field Dressing Station within the Battalion and Brigade perimeter. That evening I went to see him. He was lying on a stretcher (there were obviously no beds), being tended by his orderly, in the poorish light of a hurricane "bhutti" (lamp). He recognized me, and just said, "Sahib". I sat with him for quite a while in the gloom, saying nothing, but just letting him see that I was there. I could see that he was dying, and indeed he did die during the night.

99

After nearly four years of fighting one had come to rationalize, or at least cope emotionally, with the death or wounding, often hideously, of men for whom one had come to have a high regard, but Badshah Gul's death somehow affected me more than any other man's death in the whole war. To go through all that fighting, to survive two wounds and then, when the war was nearly over, to be killed in an accident, seemed to be a pitiless and utterly unfair turn of fate. It took me quite a few days to throw off a slough of melancholy and bitterness at the war. Even now, nearly sixty years later, I feel a great sadness.

G. Background Events

September 1945-February 1946

Shortly after VJ Day the Battalion moved from its tactical position on the
west bank of the Sittang, across that river by ferry to occupy comfortable buildings in the township of Kyaikto. Its immediate task was to
disarm the Japanese 18th Division (See map, page 14).

Chapter 20

The Surrender

In the period immediately preceding VJ (Victory over Japan) Day the Battalion was deployed about sixty miles from where it had started the Burma campaign nearly four years before, on the western bank of the River Sittang, holding ground and, at the same time, under the orders of a new gallant and thrusting Indian Cavalry Brigadier, preparing to assault across the river and seize the eastern bank. This was held, according to his Intelligence sources, by the shattered remnants of the Japanese Army which had just escaped from Western Burma through the British net. The atom bomb had been dropped; everyone other than our Brigadier was content to hold their ground and let events take their course. We therefore viewed the proposed assault river crossing with a marked lack of enthusiasm. As events were to prove, our misgivings were entirely justified, as we were facing not shattered remnants but the 18th Division, the conquerors of Singapore, which had been engaged in fighting in Central Burma, but had since been built up again. We should have had a blood bath. As it was, VJ Day came just in time. It was marked by the British front-line troops with a tremendous and spontaneous *feu de joie* along our whole front, mostly small-arms tracer but a few spectacular star shells fired by the gunners. I recall hearing that some pompous staff officer inquired of Battalion HQ what the fire was about and was given the bolshy reply, "What fire?" It was the tailend of the monsoon, with rain, damp and mud everywhere, so the euphoria of the occasion soon evaporated to be replaced by a feeling of melancholy, at the utter futility of war in which our battalion had lost hundreds of men just to finish up where we had started four years before.

There was one significant difference between the surrender of the German Army in May 1945 and that of the Japanese Army in Burma four months later. The members of the former all became individual POWs; the latter were designated JSP (Japanese Surrendered Personnel) and remained under command of their own officers in areas designated by the British. The Japanese retained responsibility for the administration and discipline of their own men, assisted where necessary by the British with food and other essential supplies such as POL and medicine. The first requirement was to move the Japanese into designated areas and disarm them.

The 18th Division were duly ordered by our Brigade Headquarters to move into an area of scrub jungle some seven miles north of Kyaikto, itself twenty miles east of the Sittang, and was promptly carried out by the Japs. They were about 10,000 strong and so occupied quite a large area, fortunately with adequate water supplies. In step with their move, my Battalion crossed the Sittang by a sapper ferry and moved into good buildings in Kyaikto. Somewhat poignantly, the ferry ran beside the shattered remains of the road/rail bridge, prematurely blown in February 1942 and leaving most of the Division on the wrong side; our Battalion had been about the last to cross before the demolition. Our immediate task was to supervise the handover of all weapons, ammunition, explosives and other warlike stores and their storage in some good godowns adjacent to Kyaikto railway station. This was to be carried out without fraternization – as stupid an order as we were ever to receive. Ever since the Japs had overrun the Battalion in 1942 and murdered all our wounded, we had fought the war cleanly but mercilessly, and the last thing on earth that we wanted to do was to fraternize with the enemy.

Dodgy and Siri went on compassionate leave and Joe Hudson and Roderick were away somewhere on other duty. Command of the Battalion was therefore temporarily in the hands of the 2IC Major B. (Brian) L. von D. Harding, "The Baron". I, as the next Senior Company Commander, actually with the Battalion, was Acting 2IC.

The Baron called me to Battalion Headquarters for a conference with him and the Acting Adjutant, Norrie Waddell, since Jimmy Whelan, the Adjutant, was also away. We decided that the first

103

thing was to decide on a priority for handing in weapons, I think it was – personal weapons, support weapons, guns, ammunition including explosives and mines, engineer stores and other warlike stores such as range-finders, binoculars and cameras. We then decided to visit the Jap Headquarters to make contact and deliver our orders. We took the practical view that to a considerable extent we needed their cooperation and this would best be achieved by a firm but dignified approach, making few concessions, but at the same time avoiding arrogance, offensiveness or inflicting deliberate humiliation for its own sake. In other words we intended to act as British Officers, not Japanese Officers. At this time we had no direct communication with the Japs and no one who could speak Japanese. We were able to get a message to them via the Brigade radio net, announcing our proposed arrival and ordering guides to meet us at a selected rendezvous at a certain time with an English-speaking interpreter. We duly set out in two jeeps.

We were punctually met by the guide and led through their area to their Divisional Headquarters. It was a very strange feeling. We had been fighting the Japanese all this time, but the only ones we had seen close up in any numbers were dead ones. We arrived at Divisional Headquarters, which was situated just below a small jungle-covered hill. As we got out there was a stentorian shout and a party of Japanese with rifles and fixed bayonets came charging down the hill. "God," I thought, "the buggers are going to have a go at us", but, to our intense relief, it was only a ceremonial guard of honour according us the honours of war. We were met by the Japanese General and his immediate staff, who were again the acme of correctness, and conducted us into their operation centre/conference room where, to our considerable relief, we met the only English-speaking Jap officer on their staff, a rather smooth, oily lieutenant, who had been at Chicago University before the war. We delivered our orders for the handover of all weapons etc, with a detailed programme, the whole thing to be completed in seven days, and we called for full lists in English of all the equipment they held to be delivered to Battalion Headquarters the next day. Additionally, except for men delivering weapons in their transport to the collecting point at Kyaikto, no Japanese were to leave their area without our permission; a telephone line was to be laid from their Divisional Headquarters to our Battalion Headquarters to be arranged under the supervision of our Signals Officer and manned by the Japanese at all times. The Japanese accepted all these without demur and we felt, "This is all too easy". However, it wasn't quite that way.

The Japs then raised the question of swords, a piece of military equipment we had not considered. It is important to realize two things; every Jap officer and warrant officer wore his sword at all times. This was not as anachronistic as it might appear. Their two-handed swords were made of the finest steel and were an extremely potent weapon in close-quarter fighting, as we had learnt to our cost; they were even strong enough for a burly Jap to hack his way through barbed wire. Secondly, the sword was the outward symbol of the individual Japanese officer's personal honour, his bushido; many were family heirlooms of superb crafts-manship and immensely valuable. The Japanese General requested that, as a matter of honour, each officer be permitted personally to surrender his sword to our Commanding Officer. The Baron, Norrie and I exchanged glances and the Baron then said that this was a matter on which he required time to consider the implica-tions. He then temporarily terminated the conference and we three withdrew to talk this new development over. After some initial doubts we decided to agree to their request, making it clear that it was a considerable concession to which we were only prepared to agree on the following conditions: swords would be handed in last and only those of officers, not warrant officers; the Divisional Commander and Regimental Commanders would have to hand their swords to our Brigade Commander; for operational reasons swords could not be exclusively handed to our Commanding Officer, and it would, at least some of the time, have to be to a British officer of field rank; and finally, and most importantly, we would only agree if all the other equipment had been handed in, fully, correctly and strictly in accordance with the timetable that we had delivered. The Japanese, with obvious relief, agreed.

We prepared to leave, but the Japanese General then invited us to move next door to accept hospitality. Again I caught the Baron's eye, but after a momentary pause he accepted and we moved into the mess. We were given some excellent saki and a certain informality descended upon the proceedings, even though I personally found it distasteful. It was on the border line of offending the rule about non-fraternization, but we were also full of soldierly curiosity as to the plans and dispositions of the 18th Division, when we had been facing them across the Sittang. Maps were produced and for about an hour some interesting professional discussions took place. We then realized how the advent of VJ Day had saved us from some extremely bloody fighting. Although there was no back-slapping camaraderie or anything approaching fraternization, it was nevertheless a fascinating experience.

The programme went ahead during the ensuing week and I have to admit that the efficiency and discipline of the Japs was first class and they met our requirements to the letter. The regimental history contains the following: "One could not but marvel at the discipline and composure of the Japanese during their humiliation; they seemed determined to carry out our every order fully, however distasteful." Finally came the sword-handing-in ceremony which had to be spread over two days. We gave considerable thought to the stage-management of this and I have to admit that our foremost concern was that at the last minute some Japanese officer, crazed with the indignity of handing over his sword, might draw it and take one of us to his death with him. We arranged a small dais with a table alongside it. Starting with the Japanese officers lined up by seniority, they would in turn approach the Commanding Officer, salute, withdraw their sword still in its scabbard from the frog or sword belt, hold it towards him in two outstretched hands, hand it over, salute and withdraw. The British officer would acknowledge both salutes and hand the sword over still in its scabbard to an orderly who would place it on a table. At no time was any Jap officer to unsheath his sword, on pain of death. Just to avoid any suicide attack, we had some hand-picked tommy gunners standing close by – mag on, one up the spout, safety catch off. At the first sign of treachery the offending Jap was to be shot and the Tommy Gunners grouped themselves around the other Jap officers. Since it was likely to be a prolonged and tiring business for the Baron, as acting CO, a roster was arranged for the other Majors to stand in, and Tommy Bruin (A Coy), Joe Hudson (D Coy), back from his duty elsewhere, and I each did a stint.

In the event the ceremony went off without incident, a strange and even moving experience, and to me personally it signified more than anything else the magnitude of our victory.

106

I can only echo the above quotation from the regimental history. Then and in the ensuing months when we used them as a labour force (they even spent hours rolling a cricket pitch for us), I came to respect the Japs for their dignity and their discipline in what must have been a time of profound humiliation.

Chapter 21

All for the Want of an Army List

Some years ago there was current an amusing parody of a well-known military maxim, which went, "Time spent in consulting the Army List is seldom wasted". Certainly in my post-Indian Army service in the Devons/Devon and Dorsets I found this to be abundantly true, particularly if one's unit was being visited by an unknown but senior officer. A quick glance at the Army (Gradation) List, a summary of officers' careers listed alphabetically, could tell one that for example he had started his military service as a gunner and had served on the British Defence Staff in Washington. An appropriate question at lunch, "I believe you served in Washington once, Sir?" would keep him happily talking about himself and how well he got on with the Americans and thus diverting his mind from probing questions about ones own unit. On the other hand failure to do one's preliminary Army List homework and the telling, during lunch, of some ill-considered and earthy infantry anecdote involving horse-copers, drop-shorts or jam-stealers, to visiting top brass with cavalry, gunner or RASC/RCT origins, could lead to military oblivion or a spell in the French Foreign Legion. This story, however, is about how, in 1945, the officers of my battalion of the Baluchis, myself included, were spared much 'taklif' by the absence of an Army List in our Brigade HQ.

After the Japanese had handed in all their weapons and equipment, as related in the previous chapter, a party of us went and examined the huge arsenal of weapons – machine guns, mortars, guns, armoured cars, etc which had been handed in – an awesome sight. It was quite noticeable that, as a result of the British defeat in Malaya and the American defeat in the Philippines, a considerable amount of British and U.S. equipment had been taken into use by the Japanese Army.

The Japanese had also handed in a number of binoculars, some cheap British and Japanese ones, but also a few high-quality German Zeiss, and some cameras, which included a few superb Leicas. All the lists were made out by the Japanese in fairly rough and ready English. One officer noticed that the Japanese had merely shown these on their lists as binoculars and cameras, by quantity but with no other detail. This seemed a golden opportunity to get some reward for four years of fighting and over the next few days some swaps of cheap cameras, which some officers had, admittedly illegally, been carrying about, took place. Fortunately also the Quartermaster was able, quite legitimately, to write off a number of British binoculars as being unserviceable, and these too were swapped.

About a fortnight later the Brigadier rang up the Baron and stated that he had had reports that our officers had been pilfering Japanese equipment, that he was extremely disturbed about this apparently disgraceful breach of discipline and that he was proposing to convene a Court of Enquiry, with a Lieutenant Colonel of another regiment as the President. How the Brigadier got his information we never knew. Battalion Headquarters was on the main divisional axis and we were open house to all who passed through. Some passing visitor had probably overheard one of us talking indiscreetly and betrayed our hospitality.

The Baron, as merely the acting CO, received this news with some dismay and called a council of war with Jimmy Whelan, the Adjutant, and me. We decided that the die had been cast and that we could only stick it out – certainly not swap our acquired treasures back.

Now the Brigadier had a battalion of the Rajput Regiment, Divisional Troops, in his brigade which was commanded by Lieutenant Colonel Brian Montgomery of the Baluch Regiment, attached to the Rajput Regiment, and the younger brother of the Field Marshal. During the war it was not unusual for battalions of infantry, both in the British and Indian armies, to be commanded by officers of other regiments. Most fortunately, however, the

Brigadier had no Indian Army list in Brigade HQ and, being a cavalry officer, was not as *au fait* with infantry officers as he was with cavalry officers and assumed that, as Brian Montgomery was commanding this Battalion of the Rajput Regiment he was a regular Rajput Officer.

Brian Montgomery duly arrived with the rest of his Court of Enquiry. He alone called in at the mess for a preliminary cup of coffee with the Baron and me. He greeted us with "Well, what have you chaps been up to?" The Baron told him the plain unvarnished truth. We certainly had swapped over some items, but strictly on a one-for-one basis, and that we had been fighting the Japanese for nearly four years and reckoned that if anyone deserved some of the spoils of war it was us. Brian Montgomery gave him a smile and left to carry out his enquiry, which he did most thoroughly, inspecting all the relevant equipment. He did not, however, call on any of our officers or men to give any evidence. On leaving he said goodbye to the Baron, not mentioning anything about the enquiry, but did give a quick wink.

Ten days later a copy of the proceedings of the Court of Inquiry arrived at Battalion Headquarters. The essential findings were that the numbers and types of equipment seen by the President and the Court of Inquiry tallied exactly with the Japanese list and that there was thus no evidence of any malpractice by any member of the Battalion. All absolutely true – as far as it went – but it could have been a very different story with another President.

I suppose that sooner or later the Brigadier discovered that Brian Montgomery had been a Baluchi, but it was too late then and, in any case, though hard, he was not a vindictive man and, after all, the Battalion did have a magnificent fighting record. The Brigadier, Brian Montgomery and the Baron are all now dead. I hope that from the halls of Valhalla they will view this little revelation with wry amusement.

(*This story originally appeared in the Newsletter of the Indian Army Association and the journal of the Devonshire and Dorset Regiment.*)

Chapter 22

Dacoits

I know very little of the history and sociological background to dacoits and dacoity in Burma. Doubtless somewhere there is a learned volume on its origins and practice. All I do know is a little about the reality of dacoits in a small area of Southern Burma, where it appears to have been endemic, both before and after the Second World War.

In this area, just to the east of the Sittang River, these dacoits were simply robber bands who attacked isolated villages and vehicles, especially buses, for what they could find. They were not generally violent for violence's sake and would only use force if opposed. They did not rape or attack their victims, nor burn or destroy properties that they had robbed; they were thus feared, but not hated. They seemed to have no political background and no connection with the Burma National Liberation Army of Aung San which co-existed with the British Army in Burma, in an uneasy truce, after the end of the war against the Japs. Whereas the Burma National Army was well armed, both with British weapons, provided by us for use against the Japanese, and with captured Japanese weapons, the dacoits' weapons were mostly the dah – the traditional Burmese weapon and tool, a long thin very sharp jungle knife used both as a weapon and for cutting bamboo shoots etc, supplemented by the odd shotgun or rifle. What I never discovered was whether a man was a professional dacoit or whether, like the traditional country poacher in England, he had a perfectly respectable daytime working occupation and only indulged in dacoity at night or on holidays, and then in an area where he would not be recognized by any of his victims. On my Battalion's arrival in Burma in early 1942, just before the Japanese invasion, there were dacoits operating throughout the country. With more serious preoccupations, we did not find them a problem, either then or in the advance back in 1945. Then in October 1945, a bare month after VJ Day, when we were taking a soldier's ease, not much military work, plenty of games and parties, leave, good hot food and undisturbed nights in bed, they started up again.

At this time normal civil government had barely had time to re-establish itself. The Burma Police was being rebuilt under a cadre of British officers, but was heavily occupied in recruiting and building up its organization, including the necessary CID and Special Branch and their intelligence network. District Commissioners and Magistrates, with their associated courts of law, were barely in existence and so, in practical terms, the maintenance of civil law and order became the responsibility of the Army, being the only formed and disciplined body in existence in the country. For a brief period each Company Commander was given the powers of a District Commissioner or Magistrate, but never used them in practice.

The dacoity took the usual form of raids on villages and on buses, just beginning to re-establish a network of services. At first these raids seemed haphazard, but gradually a picture built up of a recognizable pattern and it was discovered that they were under the leadership of a well-known pre-war dacoit, known as Na Mo. The gangs in our area were unusually vicious, killing and raping as well as robbing.

In the absence of any worthwhile intelligence our response was the rather unimaginative one of prophylatic patrolling. Surprisingly enough, in the light of the subsequent failure of such tactics in Malaya and elsewhere, these met with some success, probably due to the dacoits' over-boldness and underestimate of our strength and efficiency. Our Army then, compared with pre-war garrisons and after three and a half years of fighting, was very tough, professional and resourceful.

One day I was ordered to send a strong platoon to patrol a certain area and decided that I would go along to get to know the countryside and took Subedar Moghal Baz with me. About a couple of hours out our patrol was ambushed by a dacoit band.

112

They opened fire (fortunately very inaccurately) on me with a shotgun and then about a dozen of them came charging in wielding dahs. Against raw troops they might just have been successful, but against my battle-hardened Pathans they didn't stand an earthly. A few short bursts of accurate professional fire from Brens and Tommy guns, and a bit of deft work with the bayonet, and it was all over. I and Subedar Moghal Baz examined the scene and the latter, with all the Pathan's love of firearms, picked up the shotgun and was examining it with a gleam in his eye. "O no, Subedar Sahib," said I. "That gun was fired at me. I'm having it." Moghal Baz handed it over with a broad grin, even though the stock had been smashed by a bullet.

I got permission to keep it and when, a few months later, I was transferred to the British Army, I took it with me to join the Devons in Germany and had it re-stocked for the price of a few cigarettes. For the next 50 years or so I used it for shooting in the UK and for roughshooting in Germany. The dacoits never took us on again after that!

On another occasion we had an equally dramatic encounter. I was on a three- or four-day patrol, with Company Headquarters and two platoons, in a very remote area miles from our normal location. Under these patrol conditions I marched at the head of the column with the leading platoon commander and just a couple of scouts up in front. The country was medium thick jungle, mostly secondary, with tall trees but foliage not too thick at ground level, with the occasional rubber plantations which had fallen into disuse, interspersed with large areas of open paddy. One morning on patrol we came round the bend of the jungle track into a glen on the outskirts of a village where a civilian bus was halted. A bunch of Burmese women, several of whom were attractive, I recall, were standing, wailing and wringing their hands, whilst a gang of dacoits was ransacking the bus, completely unaware of our presence. They could have had no idea that any army units were within fifty miles.

Most of us have at some time been to a pantomime where a stage villain is caught in some act of villainy and gives an impressive display of mock horror gradually spreading over his face. One of the dacoits, looking up from rifling through some baggage, did just that; his horror and disbelief were almost laughable. He and the rest of his gang reacted fairly quickly, dropping everything and scuttling off away from us through the village. I ordered the company to spread out, 10 Platoon left, 11 Platoon right, fix bayonets and comb the village, and off we went at a soldierly double. We swept through the village and out into open paddy with the gang just ahead of us. The Rules of Engagement were not particularly well defined, but generally we only opened fire if attacked. The main aim was to capture dacoits, not to kill them. However, the fittest sepoy in the right-hand platoon outstripped the rest of us and had his bayonet into one of the dacoits, but not fatally, before I came up, and we captured the rest of them. I had orders to patrol on some time and distance ahead and did not want the burden of having to escort a bunch of dacoits whilst on patrol. I took a chance on a bit of poetic justice, took them back to the village which they had just been robbing and called for the head-man. I told him that I was proposing to leave the dacoits in his custody for a day or two. On my return I expected to find them there – and alive. This he did, and no dacoits could ever have been more pleased to see us on our return than this bunch, who were indeed alive, but had had a very hard time from the head-man and the villagers.

In a subsequent operation one of our companies, by some brilliant work, captured the dacoit leader Na Mo and handed him over for custody to the newly arrived British Superintendent of Police to be tried. Unfortunately, due either to treachery or incompetence, Na Mo escaped, which was a very disheartening blow after all our weeks of hard work, and even danger.

The Gurkha Battalion in our brigade had a marvellous idea which they called the "Q bus". The idea was taken from the Q ships of the First World War, when armed ships were disguised as harmless merchantmen, with the aim of luring a U boat (which in those days economized in the use of torpedoes by endeavouring to sink their victims by surface gunfire) within the range of their guns. When this happened the Q ship ran up the White Ensign, quickly removed the camouflage and opened fire, often with conspicuous success. The idea of the Q bus was that a party of Gurkhas armed to the teeth, would be hidden behind camouflaged sandbags. Other Gurkhas were dressed up as Burmese women and the bus then proceeded to trail its coat, until eventually they were ambushed by some armed dacoits. The panic party of "women" ran away into the jungle and the dacoits unsuspectingly ran up to the bus. At the last moment, when at point-blank range, down came the sandbags and half a dozen Gurkhas simply wrote off the dacoits with Tommy Gun fire. Of course this could only work once, but it made local bus travel a good deal safer for many weeks.

I once asked the head man of Kyaikto, the quite large town in which the battalion was located, what had happened during the time of the Japanese occupation. He told me a chilling story, though whether it was true or not, I was never able to verify. After the British withdrawal there was a brief period of freedom from dacoits, but then it started up again. The Japanese put up with this for a while, but then decided that they had had enough. They delayed an infantry regiment (three battalions), moving up towards the front, for a week and deployed them to round up every known or suspected dacoit in the area. These suspects were then brought to the centre of the town where a huge banyan tree stood. Selecting one of the known dacoits, the Japanese put a meat hook, attached to a rope, through his jaw, hauled him up into the air and left him there. It took the man two days to die and whilst he did die in hideous agony, the rest of the suspects were forced to sit and watch him. There was no more dacoity in that area throughout the Japanese occupation!

After a while our rather more humane efforts began to tell and the incidence of dacoity subsided, certainly until I shortly left the Battalion on my return to England and to the British Army. I have a feeling that, being a traditional pastime, it still goes on.

Chapter 23

Full Circle

This rag-bag of reminiscences began in February 1942 with the virtual annihilation of my Battalion by an overwhelming number of Japanese in our position on the west bank of the River Salween, an attack mounted, albeit indirectly, from Pa-an, a township on the east bank. In September 1945, following the Japanese surrender, that area was taken over by a battalion of Gurkhas in our Brigade, and their Battalion Headquarters was located in Pa-an, that self-same township, which also contained a large number of Japanese prisoners. We had been fighting alongside that battalion of Gurkhas for many months and we had all become warm friends and comrades-in-arms. In November they decided to hold their first post-war guest night and invited two of our officers as guests. Dodgy Som Dutt, the CO, decided, as a particularly thoughtful gesture, that he would send the only two officers still with the Battalion who had been there in February 1942 and suffered our bitter defeat. Accordingly Siri and I went.

We set out with mixed feelings. En route I tried to find the Burmese cultivator who, back in February 1942, had given me and my small party of survivors water and food, as we made our way back to British lines, in order to reward him handsomely. I found his bamboo hut but sadly there was no trace of him. Siri and I wandered over the scene of the battalion battle, but four monsoons and four years of tropical growth had made much of it unrecognizable. It was a melancholy business.

We crossed over the Salween to a very cordial welcome from the Gurkhas, who had established their mess most comfortably in Pa-an township. Siri and I were of course staying the night and, when we entered the Mess before dinner, their Colonel welcomed us warmly and said, "We know what you two chaps and your battalion suffered here nearly four years ago. You should know that out in the rain [there was an unseasonal deluge outside], standing rigidly to attention, are a thousand Japs. They will stand there until you give the order for their dismissal. And what would you like to drink?" I have to admit (and comparing notes with Siri afterwards he felt the same) to a slight feeling of embarrassment. Clearly the Gurkhas intended this as a special compliment to us – almost an exorcism of the ghosts of defeat and death which the place represented to us – and it would have been churlish not to have responded in the spirit in which it was intended. The Gurkhas were ever hard men.

We had several drinks and then, just before we went into dinner, we suggested to our hosts that perhaps they might wish to dismiss the Japanese, which they did. I heard later that the reason for this penance had been explained to the Japanese, that they accepted it as entirely right and proper, and that every man jack of them stood there in the rain, rigidly and unwaveringly at attention, like Guardsmen on Horse Guards, for the whole thirty or forty minutes. One could not but admire them.

Siri and I drove away from that haunted place the next morning with mild hangovers, but with a great lightness of spirit. The war was finally over.

(*This story originally appeared in* Tales from the Burma Campaign 1942–1945, *published by the Burma Campaign Fellowship Group*).

Postscript

Siri and I were the only two officers who served in the Battalion, unbrokenly, throughout the Burma Campaign. By some miracle neither of us was wounded. During the 1945 Meiktila fighting, however, when my company, mounted on the top of the Sherman tanks of our supporting squadron to move up to a start line for an attack, ran into a minefield, Company HQ, myself included, were blown off our tank; the resultant damage to my ears led to two spells in hospital and considerable deafness in later life. In my case a contributory factor to being spared was that I was Adjutant during the Chin Hills and Imphal fighting, when, the Battle of Pa-an excepted, we had our heaviest officer casualties. Whilst Adjutants did get hit, at Battalion HQ one was not quite as exposed as those in rifle companies. In Siri's case, he was on long-planned, and richly deserved, marriage leave during almost all that fighting.

Appendix A

Personalities

(References to where the individual is mentioned are shown at the end of each entry using the following abbreviations).

(Chap = Chapter: Back = Background Events: Ill = Illustration: App = Appendix) (PM is Punjabi Mussulman, VCO – Viceroy's Commissioned Officer)

1. ALI HAIDER KHAN
Company Havildar Major of B Company 1941/42. A fine looking very dutiful PM. Killed in action at Pa-an, trying to strangle a Jap in hand-to-hand fighting (Chap 2).

2. AMIR KHAN, IOM
Naik B Company. PM. The classic poacher turned gamekeeper and a real "old soldier" with an ever-mischievous twinkle in his eye. Brave to a fault. Crack Tommy Gunner. Killed in action at Pa-an winning a posthumous Indian Order of Merit (Chap 2, Back B, Ill).

3. ANDREWS D.S. (Denys)
C Company Commander from Oct 1942 until killed in action above Bishenpur on 6 June 1944. A charming man and a fine soldier (Back C, Chap 8, Ill).

4. BADSHAH GUL
Subedar. Khattak Pathan. Served throughout whole Burma Campaign twice wounded and tragically killed in an accident in June 1945. (Chap 19).

5. BAZAR KHAN
Jemadar PM. Commanded 11 Pl B Company in 1941/42. Killed in action at Pa-an. (Chap 2, Ill).

6. BRUIN T.A. (Tommy)
Joined the battalion in late 1943 and served in it throughout the rest of the war as, progressively, Company Officer to Clifford Martin in A Company, Intelligence Officer and Company Commander. A delightful Scot, who had started his service as a Trooper in the Lovat Scouts. Nothing ever seemed to disturb his calm deliberate sang-froid. After the war he worked for the Scottish Coal Board and for the London School of Economics. Still going strong at 88. He and his Swiss wife Renata have been life-long friends. (Back C, Chaps 8, 15, 20 Appx C and D and Ill).

7. BOYES T.P. (Tom)
MC Adjutant and Company Commander 1st/10th Gurkhas. After war he transferred to British Army (RASC) and finally retired to West Country. (Chap 18).

8. CAYLEY W.B. (Bill)
A Company Commander in 1941/42. Taken prisoner at Pa-an. Tea planter before and after the war. A tough, amusingly cynical man, older than most of the battalion officers. (Back A & B, Ill).

9. COUBROUGH C.R.L. (Charles)
Regimental Signals Officer 1941/2. Taken prisoner following the Battle of Pa-an after a valiant two-day attempt to get back to British lines. He showed much courage in captivity as recorded in his book *Memories of a perpetual Second Lieutenant*. We joined the Battalion on same day (20/9/41) and became friends. After the war and Cambridge, he qualified as a solicitor and was a partner in a private practice in London for many years. I was much abroad in our middle years, but he and I have become close friends (and his wife June) in our prime. We celebrated our sixtieth anniversary of meeting with an excellent lunch at the Garrick Club on 20/9/01. (Introduction, Chap 1, Back B, App C and D, Ill).

10. DAVIES A. (Tony).

B Company officer in 1945 fighting. Slightly wounded at Pegu in May and in a PIAT accident in June. A very pleasant, laid-back but efficient officer, with a passion for firing off a captured Japanese Medium Machine Gun loaded with coloured tracer. (Chap 14 & 19, Ill).

11. DUNN P.O. (Pat)

A pre-war regular officer (Dehra Dun) and Anglo-Indian. Adjutant and then 2IC in 1941. He commanded the Battalion in 1942 for a month after the Battle of Pa-an until injured and flown out of Burma. He rejoined in October 1942 as a Company Commander, and was wounded in the Chin Hills fighting in March 1944, but did not rejoin. He remained in the Indian Army after independence and retired as a Lieutenant General to live in Delhi. (Back A Chaps 3, 4, 5 & 7, Back B, Appx B, D).

12. DYER C.J. (Jerry)

Pre-war regular with much service on the Frontier, where he had been wounded. Was 2IC but took over command in Dec 1941, just before the Battalion moved to Burma. Wounded at Pa-an, taken prisoner and murdered by Japs. A proud, very brave man, who may perhaps have been a little intolerant of the failings of his very raw officers such as me. Charming in the Mess and on the golf course. (Chaps 1 & 2, Back A & B, Ill).

13. GHULAM YASIN, MC

Subedar PM. A fine, brave platoon commander whose defence of Red Hill was critical to that battle. Sadly killed shortly afterwards by our Artillery. (Chapter 8, Ill).

14. GILLETT R.H. (Dick)

B Company Commander 1941 to whose Company I went as Company Officer on joining. A very mature and impressive soldier who, thinking 7th/10th Baluch was destined for a military back-water in Iraq, had volunteered for the Indian Parachute Regiment, where he was posted in Dec 1941, thus giving me command of the Company. Killed in action in 1944 at Sangshak (Imphal) with Indian Parachute Brigade. (Introduction, Ill).

121

15. GIRDHARI LAL
Dogra Sepoy. Pat Dunn's orderly and then Company Sepoy. (Chap 4).

16. GOULDSBURY P. (Pat)
Captain and Battle Adjutant 2/5th Gurkhas during heavy fighting on Silchar Track, above Bishenpur, during Battle of Imphal 1944. After the war I met him again when he was District Superintendent Malay Police at Kulim, in Kedah, during the Malayan Emergency. In the 1960s he and his wife, Pam, ran a quail farm near Salisbury, where I was stationed, and we renewed our friendship. By a strange coincidence I had shared a room with his brother, John, 3rd/5th Gurkhas, at Bangalore. (Back D).

17. GREENWOOD O. (Bill)
B Company Officer 1941/42 who fought with me at Pa-an. Later Battalion patrol officer in the Chin Hills and Battle of Imphal. A very tough, unflappable Midlander, laid back and a great one for the girls! He had an unforgettable grin and chuckle. (Introduction Chap 7, Back B Appx D Ill).

18. HARDING L.B. von D. ("The Baron" or Brian)
A pre-war regular and Army interpreter in German and Russian. He was 2IC intermittently from late 1942 until late 1945, but was often away on intelligence jobs. A quiet, amusing but unassuming man, but a great one for a party. The 'Von D' was in memory of his maternal grandmother. (Back C, Chaps 20, 21, Ill).

19. HERRING J.K. ('Fish')
Motor Transport Officer from Oct 1942 and then Quartermaster from Oct 1944. A large cheerful and ebullient officer. After the war he was in business in the UK, but emigrated to Australia, where I had an enjoyable reunion with him and his wife Sybil at their home in the 'outback' of New South Wales in 1974. (Chap 15).

20. HOLDEN G.L.(George), MBE
One of the great characters of the battalion. He was Intelligence Officer/Machine Gun Officer at Pa-an and got away. He then

became a superb Quartermaster, who, however dangerous the fighting, never failed to get rations and ammunition up to us. An ever-cheerful, indomitable officer who was made principal administrative officer of a Brigade in the Division in Sept 1944. After the war, with his wife Thea, worked on a tea estate in Nyasaland and then, on its independence, went to Rhodesia/Zimbabwe. After her death he became a farm manager and we met there again in 1982; sadly just before we were due to meet again in 1988 he died. (Back B, Appx D, Ill).

21. HUDSON J.E.H.(Joe)
A pre-war Regular with frontier and Long Range Desert Group service. He commanded D Company from Dec 1943 to the end of the war. D Company often seemed to be involved in right flanking operations – hence "Right Hook Hudson". A tough, ever-cheerful and able officer who was renowned as a good man for a party. After the war he left the Army, married and took up potato farming in Jersey and then schoolmastering in Kent. (Back C, Chaps 8, 12, 15, 20, Ill).

22. JERVIS J.C.(Jake)
Joined Battalion in Madras in 1941 and took over D Company at the age of 19. A tall, burly, pleasant but rather self-effacing man. He was taken prisoner at Pa-an. After release he served in Indian Army until Independence, but has lost touch. (Back A & B, Ill).

23. KANTU
"Untouchable" enlisted sweeper. (Chap 10).

24. KING F.W.D.(Dizzy)
He joined in Dec 1944 and was in turn Motor Transport Officer and Quartermaster after "Fish Herring". An equable, cheerful and efficient North Country man, who never seemed disturbed from his steady calm. After the war he married Vikki and worked and retired in Swansea. (Appx D, Ill).

25. LAL KHAN
PM Subedar Company Havildar Major B Company 1941 and later Jemadar and Subedar. (Chap 1, Appx B. Ill).

26. LINDSAY P.L.(Pat)
C.O. from April 1942 to May 1944. (Chap 7 in full, Chaps 3, 4, 5, 7, 9. Back B & D, Appx D, Ill).

27. MACLEAN R.(Roderick/Mac)
He rejoined the Battalion after the Sittang River Battle from Brigade HQ where he had been Brigade Orderly Officer and served with it for the rest of the war as Adjutant in the Retreat, Signals Officer 1942–1944, Company Commander 1944, Adjutant again 1944–45. An anglicized Scot, unflappable, resolute, laconic and with a sardonic sense of humour. After the war he served in Colonial Service (Malaya) and in Hong Kong. A writer of talent (three published letters to *The Times*!). Bachelor now living in Edinburgh and engaged in writing a *History of the Cocos and Keeling Islands*. (Back B Chaps 8, 14, 15, 20, Appx D, Ill).

28. MARTIN C.F.V.(Clifford) MC AND BAR
One of the great Company Commanders, commanding A Company from Oct 1942 almost to VJ Day and involved in all the fighting except at Meiktila, when he was on well-deserved UK leave. After the war he ran the family wine business. He and I had a nostalgic visit to the Regimental Centre in Pakistan and to Siri in India in 1976. He and his wife Ridley, sadly now dead, have been close lifelong friends of mine (and my wife Peggy). (Chap 1, Back C Chaps 6, 7, 8, 14, Appx B & D and Ill).

29. MEHR KHAN
Subedar. He was my 2IC in B Company in 1941/42. A very experienced, rather laconic VCO, who, with very good reason, was not too happy being 2IC to a callow, totally inexperienced 2/Lt 19/20-year-old. Killed in action in a patrol battle at Pa-an. (Chap 2, Ill).

30. MERCER C.H.(Hugh)
He was Adjutant at Pa-an where he was taken prisoner. A very pleasant and efficient officer who after the war, in the British Army, played a big part in the reorganization of the SAS. Died as a youngish man in the 1960s. (Chap 1 Back B, Appx D, Ill).

31. MOGHAL BAZ, MC
Subedar Yusufzai Pathan. 2IC B Company in all the fighting from Dec 43 to VJ Day. A very fine soldier and a very fine man. With previous Frontier service, he was experienced, physically tough, imperturbable in battle and an excellent administrator. A devout Muslim and a man of utter integrity. Clifford Martin and I were able to visit him at his home near Mardan on the North West Frontier in Jan 1976. (Chaps 12, 13, 14, 15, 16, 17, 22, Appx B & Ill).

32. MOHAMMED KHAN
PM Subedar-Major. Oct 1942 to Oct 1944. A man of much wisdom and experience, particularly in fighting, and handling men. He played a major part in the rebuilding of the battalion under Pat Lindsay. He paid a post-war visit to the UK and lunched at my Club, to the surprise of some members. (Chap 11).

33. MONTGOMERY B.L.(Brian)
Lieutenant Colonel Baluch Regiment. Younger brother of "Monty". Commanded a Bn of 7th Rajput Regiment in our Division. (Chap 21).

34. NASIR MOHD
Sepoy. B Company Bugler and Runner at Pa-an. Killed in action there. (Chap 2).

35. PETTIGREW D.L.(Dan)
He joined 7th/10th Baluch at same time as Charles Coubrough and I. He was immediately posted to Brigade HQ as Liaison Officer. He rejoined Battalion after Sittang River Battle and commanded a company in the Retreat. He then went sick and never returned to the Battalion. (Introduction, Back B & Ill).

36. PRICE H.W.('Jock')
A classic Lowland Scot and one of the great characters. of the Battalion. Had been a Sergeant with the Highland Light Infantry in the fighting in Abyssinia and Western Desert, and so admired the Baluchis he fought beside there that, when commissioned, he came to our regiment. Intelligence Officer in Chin Hills and

Imphal fighting and Mortar Officer in 1945 fighting. Jock was utterly imperturbable, reliable and just the same whether he was fighting, partying or just doing his job. A fine soldier and comrade-in-arms. He worked for Fords in Dagenham after the war and then retired to his native Glasgow. (Chaps 7, 8, 11, Back C & D, Ill).

37. SABR HUSSAIN
PM Havildar and later Jemadar. In B Company at Pa-an A pleasant, loyal steady VCO. (Chap 2).

38. SINGHA S.C. ('Eno')
An Indian Christian Officer. Signals Officer 1944/45. A very pleasant and efficient Officer, who had a successful career in Indian Government Service after Independence. He has kept in touch over the years and attended the Indian Army Association Farewell gathering at Portsmouth in 1997. (Ill).

39. SIRI KANTH KORLA (Siri), DSO, MC
He was one of the great Company Commanders of the Battalion, taking part in all the fighting (except at Imphal when he was on long-planned marriage leave). A Dogra Brahmin, he was a regular officer (Dehra Dun) and an inspired leader, winning an immediate DSO at Pa-an. He commanded 1st Gurkhas after Indian Independence and rose to Major-General in the Indian Army. In the 1960s, as a Lieutenant-Colonel, he was the Indian Army Liaison Officer at the School of Infantry, Warminster, and came with his wife Sarla and family to stay with my wife and me in Devon. In 1976, Clifford Martin and I, having visited the Baluch Regimental Centre in Pakistan, crossed to India and stayed with him and his family in Delhi. He is alive and living in Kangra in the Himalayan foothills. (Back A & B, Chaps 11, 20, 23 & Appx B & D, Ill).

40. SOHAN LAL, IOM
He was a Dogra Subedar who served throughout the whole war in C Company. A very fine and experienced VCO. (Chaps 4, Ill).

41. SOM DUTT ('Dodgy')
Major/Lt Colonel. A pre-war regular Indian Officer who was 2IC in 1944/45. He took over command when Lt Col Wright was promoted to Brigadier. A very intelligent and pleasant man, he lacked operational experience. He stayed in the Indian Army after Independence and reached the rank of Major-General. (Back – E, Chaps 12, 14, 16, 19, 20, 23, Appx B & Ill).

42. TAJA KHAN
Havildar/later Subedar, PM. A tough, sound VCO who served throughout the whole campaign. Reliable, brave but not an inspired leader. (Chap 2).

43. TARVER G.L.(George)
A senior pre-war Regular. 2IC May-Nov 1942. A very pleasant, staff-trained officer, very helpful to me as a raw new Adjutant. He left to command a battalion of the Bihar Regiment. He was Brigade Commander of a 17 Div Brigade at Meiktila but was sacked and ironically relieved by Maurice Wright. (Back B).

44. TOOTHILL H.B. ('Toots')
Quartermaster in 1941/42. An older officer than most who had been in commerce in Madras. As Quartermaster he was only visiting battalion when Pa-an battle took place and was wounded and taken prisoner. A very pleasant, efficient officer who showed remarkable courage and endurance in surviving his wound in captivity. He returned to commerce in India after war and finally retired to the Isle of Man. (Back B, Appx 4, Ill).

45. TURNER A.P.(Tony)
Captain Motor Transport Officer in 1941/42. He was at rear details during Pa-an battle but was "Missing" at Sittang River Battle. No details ever emerged as to how he died. A pleasant, quiet efficient officer. (Back B, Ill).

46. WADDELL N.R.(Norrie)

Company Officer/Acting Adjt in 1945. A very pleasant, quietly competent member of the Scottish "contingent". Transferred to Royal Artillery in the British Army after the war and then retired to Scotland. (Chap 20, & Ill).

47. WHELAN F.J.(Jimmy)

Captain. Mortar Officer 1944 and Adjutant 1945. A very competent, ebullient officer of much charisma and a great man at a party. After the war he served in the judicial department of the Colonial Service as a Judge in Zambia and then moved to the judiciary in Western Australia. (Back C Chaps 8, 20, 21 & Ill).

48. WRIGHT M.V.(Maurice), DSO

Lieutenant Colonel/Brigadier. He took over command from Pat Lindsay in May 1944 and commanded throughout Imphal fighting and capture of Meiktila in March 1945. As a result of the Battalion's success there he was appointed to command 99 Brigade in 17 Division vice George Tarver. A highly professional operational CO, rather aloof and cool in manner off duty. After the war he retired from the Indian Army and worked for the Coal Board in the Midlands. He finally retired to Portugal. (Back D & E Chaps 7, 8, 9, 10 & 14).

Appendix B

A Nostalgic Visit to Pakistan and India by Two Old Baluchis

(This an amended and shortened version of an article first written in February 1976).

In early 1976 Clifford Martin and I paid a visit to Pakistan and India with the main aim of seeing old friends from the Battalion from the 1941–46 era. The circumstances in which the visit arose was that I, then a serving Brigadier, had to visit Muscat and Kenya on duty which involved travelling via Karachi. I therefore decided to have some leave in Pakistan/India to take up a long-standing invitation from my old regiment, and was joined by Clifford Martin, who flew direct from England to Islamabad, the new capital of Pakistan, on 23 Jan 76. Quite a lot of preliminaries had to go into organizing the trip, because it had to be cleared both with the Pakistan military authorities and their Foreign Office and with the British High Commission in Delhi. Fortunately the British Defence Attaché in Islamabad, Brigadier Georgie Powell, was a friend of mine and he went to immense trouble to lay it all on. He also acted as our host in Islamabad for a couple of days and as a launching pad for our visit.

While there we had a look round Islamabad, which had only been built some twelve years earlier and is quite an interesting example of a completely new city – clean, well-laid-out and not unattractive, but lacking the inner heart and vitality of older cities. We also had a look round Rawalpindi, including having lunch at

129

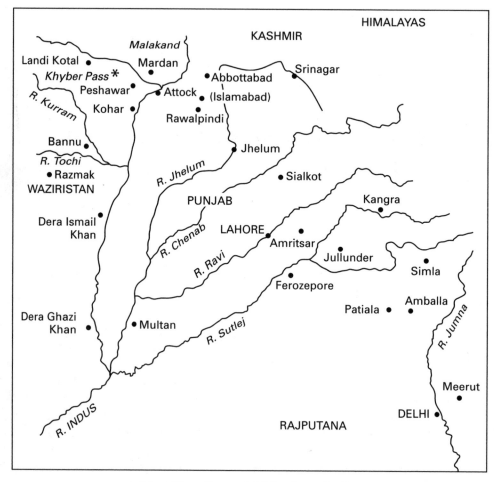

Map Six – **Imperial Northern India**

the 'Pindi club. 'Pindi itself, though neither of us had seen it in earlier times, had a somewhat forlorn look, and most things would seem to be in need of a coat of paint; this particularly applied to the bungalows on the Mall. The 'Pindi club, we imagined, had not changed very much; there was the usual crowd round the bar and an excellent curry lunch. In the afternoon we had a look round the British military cemetery, which, surprisingly enough, since it is not a Commonwealth Graves Commission responsibility, is in quite good order.

Because our visit to the Baluch Regimental Centre had something of a public relations aspect, Georgie Powell was kind enough to provide an official car for us to travel to Abbottabad, the new Regimental Centre of the Regiment, and for the rest of our time in Pakistan. Abbottabad had become a garrison town of considerable size, because it included not only the Baluch Regimental Centre but also that of the Frontier Force Regiment and the Pakistan Medical Corps plus the Pakistan Military Academy at Kakul. The Baluch Centre in fact was not in the old 5th Gurkhas Centre, which is occupied by the Piffers, but in the next-door barracks, which was, we understood, the old summer station for the Civil administration of the NWFP, North-West Frontier Province.

We were accommodated in the Baluch Guest House, in which we were given a comfortable suite of rooms near to, but separate from, the Officers' Mess, which itself had been the summer residence of the Governor of the NWFP. Though the Mess was dry, there was a bottle of excellent Scotch in each of our rooms, which was replenished daily.

We could not have been given a more warm and generous reception in every possible way, from the Commandant, Brigadier A. Q. Anjum, downwards, and throughout our two-day stay we were treated as honoured guests, with every possible courtesy and kindness. In fact the only thing that marred our stay was that it practically never stopped raining for the whole two days.

On 26 January, after a call on Brigadier Anjum, we were taken to the Junior Commissioned Officers, (erstwhile VCOs') Mess where old comrades from the wartime 7th Battalion were there to meet us. They were Subedar Lal Khan (PM) late of B Company, Havildar Clerk Mohammad Akram (PM) and Naik Haji Mohd (PM), IDSM, both late of A Company. Subedar Moghul Baz MC late of B Company had been invited, but was not physically able to make it (but see later). It was the most tremendous fun to talk to these three old comrades and, despite the rustiness of our Urdu, we soon got going reminiscing and chatting away for about two hours without a pause. Lal Khan particularly was in great form and full of fun.

That evening we were the guests of honour of the Officers' Mess, where we were received by Brigadier Anjum and all his officers. Alcoholic liquor is not served in Service Messes, but this made little

131

difference to the warmth of our reception. After a very good buffet supper we all assembled in the anteroom where Anjum made the kindest remarks of formal welcome to us and generously presented each of us not only with a Regimental tie and some very handsome regimental cufflinks, but also a beautiful inscribed silver regimental crest, in its new style of crossed swords in place of X and surmounted by a star. Fortunately we had anticipated this generosity and came bearing gifts ourselves, in the form of an original drawing-cum-watercolour picture of Subedar Khudadad Khan VC, adapted from the well-known oil painting in the Indian Army room at Sandhurst; this we presented with, we hoped, suitable words of thanks to Anjum and to the whole regiment. We then adjourned to see and hear the band play and they were indeed superb, both in their dress, green jackets and red trousers of course, and their standard of music. They were conducted by quite the most impressive bandmaster that either of us had ever seen, an enormous Pathan standing about 6'4" and as smart as any Guards Sergeant-Major on Horse Guards. Incidentally the whole of this party took place by the light of pressure lamps or candlelight, because the local power had failed, but this in effect rather added to the slightly romantic atmosphere. And so to bed, warm in heart.

Next morning we were off for a further meeting with the old comrades, including an exchange of gifts, which both sides had spontaneously brought with them, followed by a visit to the Baluch Regimental Museum which is gradually being built up with quite a number of interesting trophies from all three of the former regiments. We then attended the finals of the recruits' regimental boxing and, though this was not the greatest display of boxing skills ever seen, there was no doubt about the guts and "willingness to have a go" of all the young recruits. As a further act of courtesy, I was asked to present the prizes and was even given three vociferous cheers after a short, rather bad speech. We then went to the JCO's mess for a "barra khana" (big feast), attended by all the officers, JCOs and old comrades. This was another particularly friendly occasion and we were able to circulate round and, in our rusty Urdu, chat to those JCOs, about 50% of them, who could not speak English. We then went back informally to the Officers' Mess to have a look at the silver, pictures etc, which we had not been able to do the previous evening, because of the electricity cut.

We finally left the next morning, 28th, by paying a farewell call on Anjum and his staff to thank them for what was really a most extraordinarily heartwarming reception.

We then set off from Abbottabad to visit Captain, previously Subedar, Moghal Baz MC (Yusufzai) ex B Company, who lived in a village called Chamderi, some seven miles north of Mardan. Fortunately I had been in contact by letter with him through his son, who was a schoolmaster in Mardan. We reported to the latter, having driven through the old cantonment of Mardan, where, among other things, we saw the old Guides' Memorial, sadly in somewhat bad order. Guided by his son we set off by car towards Chamderi but, because of recent rain, could not get beyond a point some 3 miles from the village. Moghal Baz had arranged for a tonga (pony and trap) to meet us and we completed our journey to the village in that. It was a particularly beautiful, warm winter's day, with bright sunshine on the mountains up towards Malakand. We had a most pleasant four-hour stay with Moghal Baz, chatting about old times, and of course having a most excellent khana – meal. He was sporting a white beard, but apart from being somewhat lame (hence his inability to make Abbottabad) was still lively and cheerful. I was able to congratulate him on having done the 'haj' (pilgrimage to Mecca), one of his lifelong aspirations that we used to discuss during the war. As is the custom on the Frontier, a number of village elders seated themselves around us, at a respectful distance, but in earshot, and took a lively interest in all our conversation.

We then returned by tonga, picked up our car and drove to Peshawar, where we stayed in the British Embassy House, administered by an old Pathan bearer, whose first of many chittis was dated 4 April 1921!

That evening we wandered down to Deans Hotel and had an excellent meal in a somewhat deserted dining room, and then on to the Peshawar Club which does not appear to have changed very much. Anjum, at the Centre, had got in touch with Major-General Sayed Ghawas, a pre-war cadet at Sandhurst and regular Baluch officer. He retired from the Pakistan Army about 10 years ago and is now the Governor of the North-West Frontier Province, living in the magnificent Raj Government House in Peshawar. He had asked us to pay a call on him, which we duly did at 10 o'clock the next morning (29 January) and, after some reminiscing, he was kind enough to ask us to dinner that evening. We then set off on what was for us a new experience, a drive up the Khyber via Jamrud, Landi Kotal and down to Tor Khan on the Afghan border. It was a superb sunny day, with very good visibility, and the Khyber certainly looked at its most romantic best. Driving down from Landi Kotal to Tor Khan we could see right into Afghanistan and the snow-capped Hindu Kush in the distance. As we had never been up the Khyber before, we could not really make any comparisons from earlier days. The frontier-posts and forts themselves were manned by the re-raised Khyber Rifles, whose main headquarters is in Shagai Fort. Most of the old Regimental badges of both British and Indian units who served on the Khyber were maintained in very good order and it was interesting to see that Baluch badges appeared to predominate. We had a snack lunch at Tor Khan, a chat with a Naip Subedar of the Khyber Rifles, bought some chaplis in Landi Kotal and drove back for a look round the bazaar in Peshawar. That evening we went to dinner with Sayed Ghawas, who had kindly assembled a number of other Baluch officers from the Peshawar garrison. Sayed Ghawas was a most pleasant and courteous host and we had an excellent evening, culminating with him very kindly presenting us both with Wazir knives. He was "choppering" up to Razmak the next day and invited us to join him on what would have been a fascinating outing. Sadly we had to decline as we were due to return to the Punjab.

Next day we motored down the Grand Trunk Road via Attock, 'Pindi and Jhelum to Lahore, where, thanks to introductions from the British Embassy, we stayed in the new Gymkhana Club, but also used the new Punjab Club and Filettis. Fortunately we were able to see most of the famous Islamic buildings there.

On 2 February we crossed over from Pakistan to India. This was a difficult and somewhat laborious process, stemming from the then political and military situation existing between the two countries. There was no direct communication between Lahore and Delhi and the only alternative to flying via Karachi and Bombay was to cross over at a small village, called Wagha, midway between Lahore and Amritsar. This involved a car from Lahore, Pakistani porters to the midway point, a handover to Indian porters, and then, having passed through both immigration authorities, a taxi to Amritsar and the day mail to Delhi. We just had time to pay a very worthwhile visit to the famous Sikh Golden Temple, the Gurudwara.

In Delhi our most generous host was Siri (Major General Siri Kanth Korla PVSM DSO MC late 7th/10th Baluch and late GOC Delhi District). Siri had retired from the Indian Army in 1971 but had been re-employed in a civilian post as the head of Civil Defence in the Delhi area, and lived in a quarter in the old civil lines in Delhi near the Ridge. He, his wife Sarla, and his family were exceptionally kind to us and laid on a car for us to go sightseeing in and around Delhi. On 4 February Sarla and Siri organized a splendid ex-7th Baluch party, attended by (Lt General) Pat Dunn (sadly his wife Bonny had died two or three years before), and (Major General) 'Dodgy' Som Dutt and his wife. Eno Singha, late 7th Battalion, had hoped to come, but had unfortunately to call it off because he was ill. It was a most enjoyable evening. Next day Pat Dunn gave us drinks in his flat and lunch in the Intercontinental Hotel and in the evening we took Siri and Sarla out to dinner. Siri was about to retire to a very pleasant house he had bought in the Kangra Valley.

On the evening of 5 February Clifford Martin went back across the Indian/Pakistan frontier to Islamabad to fly back to England and I flew from Delhi via Bombay to Nairobi to carry on with a duty visit to Kenya.

This was an exceptionally interesting and pleasant 'pilgrimage', if one can use such a slightly pretentious term. We came away with two main impressions: firstly we were most deeply impressed and gladdened by the tremendous warmth of our reception by all Baluchis in both countries. We simply could not have been made more welcome or treated as more honoured guests if we had been royalty, and this, after 30 years of independence, spoke something for the bond which clearly existed in the old regiment and of which we were fortunate to reap the benefit. Secondly, one could not come away without a feeling of sadness about the military and political situation between the two countries.

Appendix C

Reconciliation

An Old Comrades' Reunion with a Difference

(This was written in late 1991 and first appeared in the Journal of the Devonshire and Dorset Regiment).

The Sasakawa Company, one of Japan's industrial giants, decided some years ago to set up a Foundation in Tokyo devoted to charitable work. In 1983, under the chairmanship of the late unlamented Robert Maxwell, the Great Britain Sasakawa Foundation was "established to educate the British about Japan and the Japanese and in the hope that, by bringing the two nations together in collaborated projects, a new understanding might emerge to replace the bitterness of the war years". One such project was initiated by the ABVAJ (the All Burma Veterans' Association of Japan), an organization similar to our Burma Star Association, with funds supplied by the Sasakawa Foundation. It was to invite small groups of ex-Burma British veterans to Japan as guests of the ABVAJ, with all expenses including air fares paid, with the aim of meeting a large number of their erstwhile enemies on a social basis, and at the same time showing them a wide cross-section of the country, culture and the life of the Japanese. The qualification for a formal invitation to join the group was, firstly, actually to have fought the Japanese in a fighting unit and, secondly, to go in a spirit of reconciliation. The first group went in 1989, a second in 1990, and I was invited to go in 1991. In my case, having served throughout the Burma Campaign, the first qualification was easier to meet than the second, due largely to the treatment of the wounded of my battalion when we were overrun in the Retreat from Burma in 1942. However, having thought about it and consulted my comrades-in-arms of those days, some of whom as POWs had suffered much more than I had, I decided to accept. Fifty years is a long time ago and if our late enemies were making such a major gesture of reconciliation, it seemed right at least to meet them halfway. I duly accepted the invitation for the 1991 group visit from 1 to 13 November. Our overall organization was called the Burma Campaign Fellowship Group (BCFG).

Our group consisted of twelve, eleven British ex-servicemen and a Mr Masao Hirakubo OBE. The latter had fought against us as an officer in Burma, became a convert to Christianity (RC), made his life and educated his children in England and was recently awarded the OBE by HM The Queen for his services to Anglo-Japanese relations. The eleven Brits were a wide cross-section, eight ex-Officers (three of whom were regulars) and three ex-Warrant Officers/NCOs; all but one had fought somewhere in Burma (the other being a POW from Malaya who had been on the infamous Siam-Burma railway); their postwar careers spanned being a doctor (the unofficial Medical Officer for our trip), a top British Rail Board executive, a University Don, an insurance broker, a building contractor and various posts in industry. We met for an initial briefing in London in October, where it was unanimously agreed that past ranks and titles would be discarded and we would all be on Christian name terms. We all got on extremely well and this undoubtedly added to the enjoyment of the trip.

We flew by Virgin Atlantic airlines on the afternoon of 31 October on the non-stop trans-Siberian route, arriving in Tokyo at noon the next day to be met by a welcoming Committee of Japanese veterans waving Union Jacks and bearing placards "Welcome to the British Burma Veterans" and to be warmly greeted by our hosts and housed in first-class Western-style hotels. This welcome was repeated wherever we went in Japan, even when we changed trains on one occasion. That evening we attended the first of about a dozen formal reunions, those in the evening all starting bang on 6 p.m. and all finishing, or at least the formal part, fairly soon after

137

8.30 p.m. Each of us had been warned weeks before that we would have to take it in turn to give a speech and to submit a draft so that it could be translated in advance into Japanese and read out between paragraphs of our speech in English. It was very difficult to anticipate the time, place and atmosphere of where we would eventually have to speak and most of us would have prepared different speeches if we had known when, where and to whom we would have to speak.

These reunions all had a similar pattern: initial introductions and exchanges of information about where one had fought and what British/Japanese division had been our opponents. Despite the language problem, the production of maps and photographs, plus limitless supplies of Japanese light beer, saki or whiskies and water soon broke the ice and cordial contacts were soon established. We then sat down to Japanese or occidental meals of the highest quality, off superb porcelain, deftly served by very comely kimono-clad waitresses. This was followed by speeches including that of the British veteran nominated to speak, and finally our hosts without exception produced carrier bags containing presents. Their generosity in this respect was quite overwhelming; the gifts were by no means tourist bric-à-brac, but china, jewellery, tapestries, again of the highest quality. On several occasions the final event was "Auld Lang Syne" sung in the traditional way and which apparently is as popular in Japan as it is in Britain. The most conspicuous feature of these meetings was the spontaneous warmth and cordiality of our hosts who went out of their way to be friendly and welcoming. On several occasions I could not help feeling that, irrespective of race, old soldiers are so very similar: the same steadiness of look, the same pride in their appearance, the same comradely good manners and consideration for their mates.

Our programme included two days in Tokyo, the first a Sunday, when all but two of us attended an Anglican communion service in Japanese in a Japanese church and then were taken to selected sites by members of the Anglo Japanese Society, attended a performance at the Kabuki Theatre of traditional Japanese drama and given dinner in a restaurant. The second began with a conducted tour of the City, finishing up in the early afternoon as the principal guests at the annual general meeting of the ABVAJ in a huge hall, the

Kudan Hall, filled with over a thousand members. I had drawn the short straw and to my considerable apprehension had to make the British group speech (selected because of its brevity, not its eloquence!). In drafting it weeks before I decided that I would avoid false sentiment and say nothing that I did not sincerely believe, to the effect that certain events in the Retreat from Burma had left a legacy of bitterness but that I had nevertheless admired the Japanese soldier for his devotion to duty, endurance of hardship and courage in battle, and the dignity and discipline in which he eventually accepted the surrender. This somewhat blunt approach apparently went down well and as we left the Hall by walking down the central aisle scores of old soldiers pressed towards us to greet us, shake hands and press gifts in our hands. I found it to be a most significant and moving experience. We finally went as a group to visit the Asakusa Shrine, which, with its list of all Japanese who lost their lives in Burma and elsewhere, is roughly the equivalent of our Cenotaph.

We then began a week of expertly organized sightseeing all over Japan, interspersed by receptions by the local branches of ABVAJ wherever we went. We flew to Hiroshima to see various shrines and temples and inevitably the epicentre building and peace monument at the site of the atomic explosion. Wherever we went, here and elsewhere, the general public, and especially school children showed great curiosity about us and, when it was explained to them, were as friendly and welcoming as our hosts. We then travelled by bullet train to Kyoto, the ancient capital and a treasure house of beautiful Shinto shrines and Buddhist temples. One evening there three of us enjoyed the most interesting experience of having an ordinary traditional evening meal in a traditional Japanese home, where a kimono merchant and his wife gave us a very warm and interesting welcome, a complete change from the characterless, albeit welcome, comfort of the luxury occidental style hotels in which we stayed. The next day we went via Nara and its famous giant Buddha to a most beautiful hotel on the sea at Toba with enchanting scenery, and to Pearl Island, the home of the famous Mikimoto pearls. Back to Tokyo, really to attend the Remembrance Day Service at the Commonwealth War Graves Commission at Hodogaya near Yokohama. This was a traditional Remembrance Day Service attended by the Ambassadors of the

Commonwealth countries and British residents in Tokyo.

We then went to the Hakone area, a mountainous and wooded national park of hot springs, lakes and fine scenery, overlooked by Mount Fuji. It was here that we joined our hosts in a traditional Japanese evening: all into the hot springs (though no mixed bathing), the donning of male kimonos for a traditional Japanese meal seated at low tables and then on to a karaoke for a fairly relaxed evening until the small hours.

We had two days back in Tokyo visiting the British Embassy and meeting the Defence Attachés, and attending a final reception given by the Sasakawa Foundation and a farewell party by the ABVAJ, plus a shopping expedition to the Ginza. We were finally seen off at Narita airport by our hosts for another "bum-numbing" thirteen-hour flight back, non-stop to Heathrow.

It is not easy to sum up my overall reactions to this visit. There are many who can never forgive the treatment meted out not only to British and Allied POWs, but to the inhabitants of China, by the Japanese military; others point out that Japan has never officially acknowledged its war guilt and its unprovoked and opportunist attack on British possessions in 1941. On the other hand the hospitality, kindness and generosity offered to our party was so spontaneous, so genuine and so warm that it far exceeded the normal requirement of hosts, even in Japan where the generous treatment of guests is traditional. It was not only in big things, but in many small acts of heart-touching kindness, courtesy and thoughtfulness that this became apparent. The bulk of our hosts had been front-line troops, infantry and gunners, and as one talked to them and some even showed their wounds, one could not help feeling that these were not the Kempei-tai or base troops (notorious for the fact that the further POWs in any army got from the front line the worse their treatment became), but part of that brotherhood of men (if that doesn't sound too pretentious) in any army in any war who share the rigours of being up the sharp end. There were many of our hosts for whom I felt much liking and respect and whom I would like to meet again.

It has certainly changed my perception and enlarged my understanding. I am sure that after nearly fifty years such reconciliation at that level cannot but be good. I am glad that I went and count myself lucky to have been invited.

(Note: Knowing the form, I was able to get an invitation for Tommy Bruin and Charles Coubrough to go on subsequent visits to Japan; unfortunately Charles had to cry off for family reasons, but Tommy went).

Appendix D

7th/10th Baluch Postwar

The Baluch Officers' Dinner Club

PRESIDENT BRIGADIER J.P. RANDLE OBE MC

CHAIRMAN MAJOR F.A. ROWLEY CMG OBE MC

On Indian Independence in 1947 the Baluch Regiment was allocated to Pakistan and so sadly the Dogra Brahmin element was drafted to the 17th Dogra Regiment, which was allocated to India. The 7th Battalion was retained in the regular Pakistan Army, though there was a renumbering of battalions.

The camaraderie which existed among the officers of the battalion continued down the years. For many years, as well as being strong supporters of the main Baluch Regiment Officers' Dinner Club, we had our own little battalion "dinner club", meeting annually in London for a few "starters" at the Junior Carlton or a pub, before going on to a curry supper in an Indian restaurant (Shafis in Gerrard St for many years). Pat Lindsay, our much-respected old Commanding Officer, was a staunch supporter. It was a great encouragement to me too as Chairman, and later President, of the main Baluch Officers' Dinner Club for twenty-five years, to have a lot of old friends in support at meetings and social events.

In February 1992 we had a special anniversary dinner with our wives at the Army & Navy Club to commemorate the 50th anniversary of our initial and disastrous battle at Pa-an on 11/12 February 1942. Present were Tommy and Renata Bruin, Charles and June Coubrough, Bill and Charmain Greenwood, 'Dizzy' and Vikki King, Roderick Maclean, Clifford and Ridley Martin and John and Peggy Randle. Though I presided, the principal speaker, and rightly so, was Charles Coubrough, who in 1942 had made such a valiant but sadly unsuccessful attempt to get back to British lines and who had endured, with quiet courage, over three years of arduous captivity, as recorded in his moving book *Memories of a perpetual Second Lieutenant*.

With his permission I am including the text of that speech, since it makes a fitting epilogue to my stories.

Ladies and Gentlemen

I feel very honoured to be asked to speak at this dinner when we are commemorating not only the 50th Anniversary of the Battle of Pa-an but also the very fine achievements of 7 Baluch over the subsequent three years of warfare against the Japanese, in which I was the only one of the Baluchi Officers present to play no part.

I would like to thank you John for the most generous terms in which you have introduced me.

John Randle, Bill Greenwood and I are the only survivors of the Battle present tonight. Sadly Pat Dunn, George Holden and Hugh Mercer are no longer with us.

In his letter last May suggesting this dinner, John wrote that the Battle of Pa-an was arguably the most famous Battle fought by 7 Baluch but it was the least successful in terms of military success. I agree with him. The Battle of Pa-an was a comprehensive defeat. To pretend otherwise would in my view diminish the remarkable achievements of Pat Lindsay and those Officers who served with and after him in rebuilding 7 Baluch into what became as John has said one of the finest Battalions in Burma, playing a significant part in several victories over the Japanese.

Despite the defeat of 7 Baluch at Pa-an by what was unarguably a better-trained, vastly more experienced, formidable Japanese force with complete air superiority, which they had exploited in low-level bombing attacks on our position in previous days, there are I believe many reasons why it is appropriate to commemorate the 50th Anniversary of the Battle of Pa-an.

Foremost of all is the fact that in the Battle in the early hours of the morning of 12 February 1942, 50 years ago today, some 550 Officers, VCOs and men of 7 Baluch were killed or became prisoners of war of the Japanese. There were many more killed than taken prisoner, and of these many did not survive the War.

I will not attempt to describe the Battle. Because it mainly took place in darkness, because of the nature of the terrain with its areas of thick jungle and because we were overrun by the Japanese in the end, I have really never known all that took place. But I do want to mention some fine performances which, either from my own observation or from talking to survivors, I know are true.

The brunt of the Japanese Attack when it came at about 1.00 a.m. fell up Siri's C Company of Dogras, who put up a magnificent fight. As most of you know Siri was awarded the DSO for his conduct during the Battle. John did circulate copies of a letter from Siri from India in which he wrote how 'very very happy and much thrilled' he was to receive the invitation to this dinner and conveyed his 'heartiest congratulations and good wishes' to all Officers attending.

The Japs also attacked B Company commanded by John Randle with Bill Greenwood as his Company Officer. B Company had been depleted by the loss of two platoons, one annihilated by the Japs the night before to the south where the Japs had crossed the Salween in force and the other out on patrol. They stood their ground and put up a fine fighting performance until they were overrun.

One of the survivors of the Battle is Toots, Captain Bruce Toothill, the Quartermaster, now 84 years of age and unable to travel from the Isle of Man because of his old leg wound. After the Battle was over he and Subedar-Major Kirpa Ram, a splendid formidable soldier, with a small party were trying to reach the road to Duyinzeik when they ran into some Japs. In the ensuring engagement the Subedar-Major, a powerful

144

man, was killed grappling with a Jap and Toots was severely wounded. I believe that he was the only one of our wounded taken prisoner by the Japs at Pa-an. With next to no medical attention it is remarkable that he is alive today.

Lastly, I would like to pay tribute to the CO, Lt Colonel Jerry Dyer, who was killed at Pa-an. I personally witnessed his exceptional courage and his total indifference to enemy fire.

There were, I am sure, many other brave performances in the jungle which went unwitnessed by any survivor. But I hope that I have said enough to show how right we are to mark the 50th Anniversary of the Battle of Pa-an and to remember the many comrades and friends who died there.

Index

All Baluchis mentioned in the stories are listed alphabetically at Appendix A and are therefore not included again here.

149